Baseball's
Best
101

Base
Best

Rankings of the Skills, the Achievements and the

ball's 101

Performance of the Greatest Players of All Time

Derek Gentile

Timothy Cebula, Jack Passetto and Brian Sullivan, contributors

Tess Press

Published by Tess Press, an imprint of
Black Dog & Leventhal Publishers, Inc.

Manufactured in the U.S.A.

Cover design by Liz Driesbach
Interior design by Liz Trovato

Photographs courtesy of Transcendental Graphics, AP Wide
World, Baseball Hall of Fame Library, Cooperstown, NY.

ISBN 1-57912-555-7

h g f e d c b a

Contents

Introduction

The inspiration for this book was all the lists that came out, on ESPN and elsewhere, in the year 2000 that ranked the greatest athletes of the millennium. I was intrigued by the various attempts to equate football players with swimmers, golfers with runners, and baseball players, all from different eras, with one another.

My original idea was to list the best baseball players, ever, regardless of where, when or in what league they played, including players from the Negro League, Japanese league, Cuban league and even female professionals. But, as the project took shape, I realized that, try as I may, I could really only manage to list major league players. If players from different eras are difficult to compare, then equating players from different countries and of a different sex seemed nearly impossible. In the end, though, I did make the decision to include as many Negro League players as possible.

Once I'd made my decision to narrow the focus, creating a big-league list, which included Negro league players, seemed more manageable. But, the problem now was how to compile the list. As is often the case with projects I do, I went about the process backwards. Rather than, say, start at number one and move on from there, I started with everybody who was eligible and pared it down. There are about16,000 listings in the *Baseball Encyclopedia*, and another 4,000 or so in James A. Riley's *Biographical Encyclopedia of the Negro Baseball Leagues*. So, I had a lot of work to do!

The problem was, I needed some baseline for comparison. The biggest difficulty was that stats for many of the players in the Negro League were not as complete as those figures for the major-league players. So any comparisons based purely on statistics were, alas, not going to be fair. But, to create this list based on subjectivity seemed silly. So, there had to be some baseline comparisons that could be made.

And, as a matter of fact, there were. I thought about what made great players great. Two things jumped out: consistency and durability.

Durability was a snap. I pulled out all the players who had played 10 or more seasons. The second half of the equation, consistency, meant players who were consistently good, obviously. So, I eliminated pitchers with losing records and everyday players who hit less than .260 for their careers. Then, I compiled what I called the "subjective list." This is the list of All-Star game participants, MVP winners, Gold Glove winners, and winners of individual statistical championships including batting championships, home run, RBI, runs scored, stolen bases, on-base percentage and hits leaders. For pitchers, it was won-loss percentage, strikeouts, complete games, saves, appearances and ERA.

I gave less weight to Hall-of-Famers than some others might. This is because the Hall of Fame tends to look at players from earlier eras in a more subjective way than I would have liked. I have no quarrel with the way it's done in Cooperstown, and in fact, the folks at the Hall of Fame are among the most accommodating people on earth. But this was, my list and my rules and I just thought it would be better that way. For historical reference, I did list players when they were inducted into the Hall.

I believe the Negro League players are underrepresented, but I don't know how it can be helped. I had some statistical data on all these players, and a number of texts that helped. But in the end, I excluded a lot of Negro League players because I found myself relying too much on anecdotal information.

Finally, I peeked at other lists. *Total Baseball* has a list of the top 500 major league players. The Baseball Hall of Fame has a *Baseball Desk Reference* that lists the top 700 players. And, the *Bill James Baseball Abstract* has a list of the top 100 players at each position. I compared my list to theirs to see which players I might consider tweaking up or down. Some players did get a tweak. In fact, I probably tweaked more than I should have. Looking at this final list, which believe it or not is probably the 100th version, there are some guys who, on some days, still don't look to me like they're in the right spot. But this is the list. I don't know how close it is to any list another reader or baseball fan would come up with. As I said, it's my list.

Final note:
This book was originally published to include baseball's best 1,000 players of all time. This special new edition has reorganized the list to include only a select 101 players from 1950 to the present, as well as two top-ten lists that name the best pitchers and position players from 1900 to 1950.

1. Willie Howard "Say Hey Kid" Mays, OF-1B, Giants, Mets, 1951–73. Hall of Fame, 1979.

The complete baseball player, Mays could run, field, hit for average and hit for power. There are certainly some who might put him ahead of Ruth as an everyday player.

Mays was originally a star in the Negro Leagues, playing a couple of years with the Birmingham Black Barons. His contract was purchased by the New York Giants in 1950.

Mays was one of the sparks for the Giants in that year's thrilling pennant race. Mays hit .274 with 20 home runs as the Giants won the flag. Mays was in the on-deck circle when Bobby Thompson hit his historic home run.

Mays was a 20-time All Star, and after 1954, he never missed more than five games a year until 1967. He hit 660 home runs and batted .302 for his career (take out those last three awful years, and that average is up to .311). He stole 338 bases. He won 11 Gold Gloves.

He is best remembered for a defensive play, his astounding catch off Cleveland first baseman Vic Wertz in the 1954 World Series. Wertz drilled a deep shot off Giants' reliever Don Liddle. The ball sailed into center field. But Mays tracked it down 425 feet from home plate and made an over-the-shoulder catch that is still regularly seen on highlight films.

Mays won MVP awards in 1954 and 1965. There are at least three other years in which his statistics are comparable to or better than those years, but the fact is, baseball writers were always uneasy awarding too many MVP awards to one player. Oh well.

LIFETIME STATS: BA: .302, HR: 660, RBI: 1,903, H: 3,283, SB: 338.

2. Mickey "The Commerce Comet" Mantle, OF-1B-SS, Yankees, 1951–68. Hall of Fame, 1974.

Mantle was a man blessed with thunderous home run power and blazing speed. He was named after Hall-of-Fame catcher Mickey Cochrane, and he was even better than Cochrane.

Where to start? He was a switch-hitter who hit 536 home runs: 373 from the left side of the plate, 163 from the right. With his great upper body strength, some of those home runs were monster shots, like the one on May 22, 1963, which almost carried out of Yankee Stadium.

But he was also a tremendous bunter and base stealer. Mantle stole 153 bases, including 21 in 1959. He was only caught stealing three times that year. With his speed, he also hit 72 career triples, leading the league with 11 in 1955.

Mantle, a 16-time All Star, won the Triple Crown in 1956, with 52 home runs, 130 RBI and a .353 batting average. He won the MVP award that year, as well as in 1957 and 1962. He also won a Gold Glove in 1962. He was as fast afield as he was on the base paths, and had a rocket arm.

He was a clutch player, who regularly played in pain. He was also a great teammate who befriended rookies and marginal players throughout his career. He was a leader on the Yankees and a huge fan favorite throughout his career.

He may have hung in with the Yankees a few years too long, at least by some folks' standards. But let's face it: The Mick loved the game, and it was hard to let go.

LIFETIME STATS: BA: .298, HR: 536, RBI: 1,509, H: 2,415, SB: 153.

3. Theodore Samuel "Ted," "Teddy Ballgame," "The Kid," "The Splendid Splinter," "The Thumper" Williams, OF, Red Sox, 1939–42, 1946–60. Hall of Fame, 1966.

It is hard to believe that Ted Williams, a man who was so much larger than life, is no longer with us. We want him to be like those actors on the silver screen: undaunted, immortal, unconquerable.

He wanted to be known as the greatest hitter who ever lived. He might have been. He didn't hit for as much power as Babe Ruth (although he lost four years to two wars, and still hit 521 homers). He didn't make as many hits as Ty Cobb (although his career on-base percentage is almost 50 points higher: .482 to .433).

Five times in his career, in fact, Williams had an on-base percentage of .500 or better. The year he hit .406, it was .553, a record at the time. That meant that 55 percent of the time, when Williams came to bat, he at least made it to first base. He was as nearly unstoppable as a player could be.

He played hard every game. He played on great Red Sox teams, in the late 1940s, and he played on awful Red Sox teams in the 1950s. He hit .406 in 1941, two numbers every baseball fan worth his salt knows. He hit .400 two other times, albeit in shortened seasons: In 1952 he hit .400 in the first six games of the season and went back into the service to fight in the Korean War. He came back from that war late in 1953 and hit .407.

He was an authentic American hero who fought in World War II and the Korean conflict. His plane was shot down in the Korean War and he almost died. But Williams didn't want to sit on an Army base and play on a club team: He wanted to be where the action was.

He won six batting titles, two MVP awards, four home run crowns, a Triple Crown in 1942 and was a 17-time All Star. He was a great player. When he was elected to the Hall of Fame, he used his acceptance speech to lobby for the great players of the Negro Leagues to be inducted. And soon, of course, they were.

LIFETIME STATS: BA: .344, HR: 521, RBI: 1,839, H: 2,654, SB: 24.

4. Stanley Frank "Stan the Man" Musial, OF-1B, Cardinals, 1941–63. Hall of Fame, 1969.

Consistency, durability and affability were the hallmarks of this man, the greatest player in a storied St. Louis Cardinal history.

In fact, the consistency of Stan the Man was taken to an amazing extreme: Musial had 1,815 hits at home and 1,815 on the road. He scored 1,949 runs and drove in 1,951.

His nickname, "Stan the Man" was a token of respect, bestowed on him by awed Dodger fans in the 1940s, as Musial led the Cardinals to four pennants in five years from 1942 to 1946. Musial, like the vast majority of his fellow ballplayers, didn't play in 1945, as he was in the Navy.

Dodger hurler Preacher Roe summed up his pitching strategy against Musial succinctly: "Throw him four wide ones and try to pick him off first base." Roe was only half-kidding.

Musial was a hittin' fool. He won seven batting titles, and led the league in hits six times, doubles eight times, triples five times, RBI twice, slugging percentage six times and walks once. In 1948, he missed the Triple Crown by a single home run. He was MVP three times and finished second four other times.

He was a 20-time All Star, and he probably should have made the All Star team in 1942, when he hit .315 with 32 doubles and led the Cardinals to a stunning five-game upset of the New York Yankees in the World Series .

He was a man who understood the gift he had, and appreciated it deeply. He never questioned umpires' decisions and always seemed to enjoy the game.

He played in St. Louis for 22 years, and following his stint as a player, worked in the Card front office for another 25. After his career, the city erected a statue of Musial outside Busch Stadium. It was the least they could do.

LIFETIME STATS: BA: .331, HR: 475, RBI: 1,951, H: 3,630, SB: 78.

5. Joseph Paul "The Yankee Clipper," "Joltin' Joe" DiMaggio, OF, Yankees, 1936–51. Hall of Fame, 1955.

Joe DiMaggio might have been the best ballplayer ever, and the reason he isn't even farther up the list has more to do with the era than the man.

There is no way to measure what might be called the "woulda, shoulda, coulda" factor in sports. In this case, there is no way to determine how much his three-year participation in World War II affected Joe DiMaggio's stats.

Put it this way: It didn't help. Joltin' Joe went into the service at 28 and came out when he was 31. He was an MVP twice before he went into the service, in 1939 and 1941, and once after, in 1947. He won two batting titles, both prior to 1942, in 1939 and 1940. In short, before Hitler shouldered his way into the equation, DiMaggio had a heck of a run.

And let's face it, he still put up numbers. His 56-game hitting streak in 1941 is the one record that we'd be hard-pressed to see exceeded in the modern era. His .325 lifetime batting average is 41st all-time. Four times in his career, in 1937, 1939, 1940 and 1948, he had more RBI than games played.

He almost never struck out. For his career, DiMaggio whiffed 369 times, which is 2,228 times fewer than Reggie Jackson

In the field, he saved the Yankees a lot of money in dry cleaning bills. He was almost never out of position, so rare is the old-time Yankee fan who can recall DiMaggio ever having to make a diving catch or a lunging grab. He was always right there when the ball was hit to him.

DiMaggio didn't really glide; former teammates recall a guy who ran like a buffalo in the outfield, with a thundering step and a good amount of huffing and puffing. But that was only close up. Watching from the stands, Joe made it look easy.

LIFETIME STATS: BA: .325, HR: 361, RBI: 1,537, H: 2,214, SB: 30.

6. Henry Louis "The Hammer" Aaron, OF-1B-DH, Braves, Brewers, 1954–76. Hall of Fame, 1982.

The first name in baseball, literally. Aaron's name is the opening entry in the baseball encyclopedia and that is somehow fitting.

A self-effacing star who was, except for perhaps Lou Gehrig, the most stunningly consistent player ever, Aaron showed emotion only once on the field: when he cried after he broke Babe Ruth's home run record. On April 8, 1974 against the Los Angeles Dodgers in Atlanta, Aaron belted a pitch from Al Downing over the left-field fence into the Braves' bullpen to give him 715 career home runs, one more than Ruth.

Those tears were probably at least partly of relief. It may have been 1974, but this was still Atlanta, the heartland of the South, and Henry Aaron was a black man trying to outdo a white man, who was the all-time baseball legend, to boot.

Aaron's performance under such conditions—he and his family received an incredible amount of hate mail—was remarkable. After hitting number 715, Aaron continued to play for two more years after 1974, and finally ended up with 755 for his career.

His consistency was numbing. Twenty-three consecutive years hitting 10 or more home runs, leading the league four times. Twenty-two consecutive years with 10 or more doubles, leading the league four times. Twenty-one years with more than 100 hits, twice leading the league. He was named to the All Star team 21 consecutive times. He went fourteen years hitting over .300, winning batting crowns in 1956 and 1959. He garnered three consecutive Gold Gloves. And how about this? He went nine straight years stealing 15 or more bases. Not too shabby.

Aaron remains baseball's top home run hitter, and the top man in RBI, total bases and extra base hits.

LIFETIME STATS: BA: .305, HR: 755, RBI: 2,297, H: 3,771, SB: 240.

7. Robert LeRoy "Satchel" Paige, RHP, Birmingham Barons, Baltimore Black Sox, Cleveland Cubs, Pittsburgh Crawfords, Kansas City Monarchs, New York Black Yankees, Satchel Paige's All Stars, Memphis Red Sox, Philadelphia Stars (Negro Leagues), Cleveland Indians, St. Louis Browns, Kansas City Royals, 1926–65. Hall of Fame, 1971.

Satchel Paige was one of the few legends who might have been better than some of the stories told about him. A Negro League mainstay from 1926 until 1946, Paige was a gangly man who threw a blistering fastball for most of his career.

And the stories are true. He once walked the bases loaded with no outs and struck out the side (although it was in a semipro tournament). Several times, he would call in his outfielders and pitch to an opponent, again always in exhibitions or semipro games.

Once, in a tournament in Denver in the 1930s, Paige called in his outfielders and struck out the first two batters. The third batter slapped a soft fly ball to center field that would have easily been caught had there been anyone out there to catch it. The batter raced around the bases for an inside-the-park home run.

Paige estimated that in his total career which often included playing exhibitions and playing in several leagues in one year, he pitched in 2,600 games, won 1,800, and threw 300 shutouts and 55 no-hitters.

Paige didn't like his nickname much. He earned it when, as a young boy, he tried to steal a satchel from a man at a train station. He was caught and cuffed in front of his friends, who gleefully gave him the name. Over the years, he made up several more colorful stories that better fit his status as a great pitcher.

His frequent pay disputes with the various managers of teams in the Negro Leagues caused Paige to jump teams on almost an annual basis. In 1938, he was banned from the Negro National League, so he formed his own independent team, Satchel Paige's All Stars, which easily outdrew other Negro League franchises. Paige was readmitted the next year.

In addition to his fastball, Paige had tremendous control and, like former Red Sox great Luis Tiant, possessed a variety of windups to deliver the baseball. In 1948, he was signed by the Cleveland Indians and went 6-1 as Cleveland won the world championship. He played for several more years before retiring to semipro teams and exhibitions. In 1965, he returned to the bigs, pitching three scoreless innings for the Kansas City Royals to become, at age 59, the oldest pitcher ever in the majors. It was one last story for the legend.

LIFETIME STATS (MAJOR LEAGUES): W: 28, L: 31, Sv: 32, ERA: 3.29, SO: 288, CG: 7. (Negro Leagues) W: 142, L: 92.

Compact and powerful, Joe Morgan was the National League's greatest second baseman.

Morgan broke in with the Houston Astros and played nine years in the Astrodome, making two All Star teams. He was traded to Cincinnati and developed into a superstar. Morgan was one of the keys to the Cincinnati "Big Red Machine" of 1972–76. The Reds won three National League pennants in that span, and back-to-back World Series in 1975 and 1976.

Not coincidentally, Morgan picked up a pair of MVP awards in that span, as well. Morgan is the only second baseman in baseball history to win consecutive MVPs.

An extremely patient hitter, Morgan led the National League in walks four times, and eight times in his career walked more than 100 times a year. He also led the league in on-base percentage four times.

Known for the distinctive flapping motion of his back elbow in the batter's box, Morgan had very good power for a second baseman, hitting 27 home runs in 1976 and becoming that year only the fifth second baseman in major league history to drive in more than 100 runs with 111 RBI.

He was also an exceptional base stealer, swiping 20 or more bases 14 times in his career.

But beyond his stats, Morgan was a winner. He hit the game-winning single in the 10th inning in Game Three against the Red Sox in the 1975 World Series. And in Game Seven, he struck again, dropping in an RBI single in the top of the ninth to give the Reds the championship. Against the Yankees in the 1976 World Series, he hit .333 in a four-game sweep.

In 1980, Morgan was traded back to Houston, and helped the Astros win the division title. After a two-year stint with the Giants, he signed with the Phillies in 1983 and was helped that team get into the World Series. Morgan led the team with five hits and two home runs, but the Phillies lost to the Baltimore Orioles in five games.

LIFETIME STATS: BA: .271, HR: 268, RBI: 1,133, H: 2,517, SB: 689.

Speed, power and patience have combined to make Barry Bonds the greatest hitter of his generation. Also the most under-appreciated, at least outside the confines of San Francisco.

Bonds has put up some tremendous numbers since he came to the Giants in 1993. Everyone thought he would never top his 2001 season, when he hit 73 home runs to obliterate Mark McGuire's 70-home run record in 1998. Bonds also set a single-season record with a slugging percentage of .863 that year, shattering Babe Ruth's 1920 mark of .847.

Career year, right? Well, maybe. But Bonds came back the next year and set a major league record for walks with 198 and another all-time major league record for on-base percentage, .582, breaking Ted Williams's mark set in 1941.

Bonds is only the second player in baseball history, along with Jimmie Foxx, to have hit 30 or more home runs in 13 seasons.

He is an excellent base-stealer, with 500 career swipes, although he has tapered off over the past few years.

He's a six-time Most Valuable Player and has won the last three National League MVPs in a row. An eight-time Gold Glove winner, he is a 12-time All Star and was named Player of the Decade by the Sporting News in 2000.

Bonds is one of the best clutch players in baseball, hitting a career .468 with a man on third base.

If there is one mark against him, it's that Bonds's

team, the Giants, has not won a World Series. But Bonds could not have done more in his single appearance in the 2002 Fall Classic, hitting .471 with four home runs and six RBI over the course of the Series.

He's headed for the Hall of Fame, certainly. Lately, the talk of his possible steroid use has come up again. That rumor has been around for several years now, but it remains unproven.

LIFETIME STATS: BA: .297 HR: 658 RBI: 1,742 H: 2,595 SB: 500.

10. Michael Jack Schmidt, 3B, Phillies, 1972–89. Hall of Fame, 1995.

Great hitting always overshadows great defense. That's a fact, and that's why it's so important to emphasize that while Mike Schmidt might not be as acrobatic a third baseman as Brooks Robinson or Graig Nettles, he was probably a better overall fielder.

But let's talk about hitting first, because first and foremost, Mike Schmidt was an offensive machine. He led the National League in home runs eight times, in RBI four times and in slugging percentage five times.

He had an early problem with strikeouts, whiffing a league-high 180 times in 1975. But Schmidt eventually became more selective at the plate, and four times in his career, led the league in walks.

On July 17, 1986, Schmidt hit four home runs in one game, as the Phillies rallied from a 13–2 deficit to defeat the Cubs 18–16 in 10 innings. He hit his first home run off Cub starter Rick Reuschel and his fourth off Cub reliever (and Rick's brother), Paul Reuschel.

He was also a smart base runner. He stole 174 bases in his career, and twice swiped 20 or more. He won MVP awards in 1980, 1981 and 1986. He was also the MVP of the World Series in 1980, hitting .381 with two home runs and seven RBI in Philadelphia's win over the Royals.

In the field, Schmidt was a 10-time Gold Glove winner. In 1974, he set a National League record for third basemen with 404 assists. Three years later, his 396 assists were the second-highest single season total in major league history.

He was also tough to keep out of the lineup. Until a season-ending rotator cuff injury in 1988, Schmidt played in 145 or more games in 13 of his 16 full seasons in the league.

LIFETIME STATS: BA: .267, HR: 548, RBI: 1,595, H: 2,234, SB: 174.

11. Rickey Henley Henderson, OF-DH, A's, Yankees, Blue Jays, Padres, Angels, Mets, Mariners, Red Sox, Dodgers, 1979–2003.

Henderson was the greatest leadoff hitter in baseball history, and one of the best outfielders, ever, as well.

His numbers are prodigious. Henderson is the all-time leader in walks with 2,190, breaking Babe Ruth's record on April, 25, 2001. (Henderson led the league in walks four times in his career, and was in the top five eight other times.)

Later that season, on September 28, 2001, Henderson broke Ty Cobb's all-time record for runs scored when he crossed home plate for the 2,247th time. Henderson now has 2,295 career runs scored. When you break records by Babe Ruth and Ty Cobb in the same year, you are good.

Henderson is also the all-time leader in stolen bases, a record he broke more than a decade ago, in 1992. Henderson ended his career with 1,406 stolen bases. Lou Brock, in second place, has 938.

Henderson is the only player to steal more than 100 bases more than twice, doing it three times in his career. In 1982, he stole 130 bases, setting the modern major league record. (Hugh Nicol of the Cincinnati Red Stockings of the defunct American Association stole 138 bases in 1887.)

Henderson stole 108 bases in 1983 and 100

bases in 1980. He led the league in stolen bases 12 times, including seven times in a row from 1980 to 1986.

He has hit 79 leadoff home runs, another record. That sum is more than the next two players combined, Brady Anderson (44) and Bobby Bonds (34).

Henderson is also one of the most adept players in major league history at getting hit by a pitch, doing so 98 times in his career, which places him 56th on the all-time roster.

His speed enabled him to be a very good defensive outfielder. Henderson won only one Gold Glove in his career, but he is sixth all-time in putouts in the outfield with 6,466.

Henderson may have lost a few points with purists with his "snap" catches in the outfield. This was a move where he whipped his glove across his head to grab a fly out.

Henderson was a clutch player in the postseason. He hit .339 in 14 World Series games.

LIFETIME STATS: BA: .279, HR: 297, RBI: 1,115, H: 3,055, SB: 1,406.

12. Jack Roosevelt "Jackie" Robinson, 2B-3B-1B-OF, Dodgers, 1947–56. Hall of Fame, 1962.

Yes, yes, yes, Jackie Robinson broke the color barrier in 1947, became an icon and a hero to every African-American boy of the next generation and paved the way for baseball as we know it now.

But what sometimes gets lost in all this is that Robinson was a really, really good baseball player.

Robinson was, in fact, one of the greatest athletes in the history of sport, any sport. Jim Thorpe may have been slightly better, but not by much.

For example, Robinson averaged a hard-to-fathom 11 yards per carry as a running back in his junior year at UCLA. He was the leading scorer in the Pacific 10 in basketball for three years running. He won the 1940 NCAA long jump championship, and was slated to go to the Olympics, had they not been cancelled that year. He also won both the singles and doubles titles in the Western Tennis Club championships.

He was recruited by Dodger general manager Branch Rickey to spearhead the long-overdue integration of baseball in 1946 and began playing in major league ballparks in 1947. Robinson endured extraordinary abuse from fans and opponents, yet held his emotions in check. He retaliated with a superb rookie season and was named Rookie of the Year. The rest, as they say, is history—American history, not baseball history.

Robinson was a superior base runner, perhaps the best ever. He stole home 19 times in his career. In 1955, he became one of only 12 players in baseball history to steal home in a World Series game. In 1954, he became the first National League player in 26 years to steal his way around the base paths. He was probably the best player in history at finding a way to return to base safely after being caught in a rundown.

Robinson was a good hitter, winning a batting title in 1949 and topping .300 six times in his career. He didn't strike out much and averaged about 75 walks a season.

Defensively, he led the National League three times in fielding average at second base, and was also a very good defensive third baseman and left fielder. Robinson wasn't flashy; he didn't make the diving stab. Rather, he played very intelligently, and was usually in the right place at the right time.

At his death in 1972, his former teammate Joe Page spoke for all the black players then in the league, and in fact all the black players to come in the history of baseball when he said, "When I look at my house, I say, 'Thank God for Jackie Robinson.'"

LIFETIME STATS: BA: .311, HR: 137, RBI: 734, H: 1,518, SB: 197.

13. Frank Robinson, OF-DH, Reds, Orioles, Dodgers, Angels, Indians, 1956–76. Hall of Fame, 1982.

Frank Robinson was one of the great power hitters of the 1960s. He was also a leader in the clubhouse, which was a rarity for a black man in the late 1950s and early 1960s.

Robinson made an immediate impact on the National League with the Cincinnati Reds in his first year, hitting 38 home runs, then a record for a rookie player. He also led the National League with 122 runs scored and was hit by pitches 20 times, another rookie record. For the next 10 seasons, Robinson was "the Man" in Cincinnati.

In 1961, Robinson led the Reds to the team's first pennant in 21 years, although Cincinnati had the misfortune of playing the Roger Maris-Mickey Mantle Yankees in the World Series. Robinson won the first of two MVP awards that year, hitting .323, slugging a league-leading .611 with 37 home runs and 124 RBI.

Robinson's aggressive play often led to nagging injuries, although he rarely sat down for any long stretch. Still, Reds officials believed he was losing his effectiveness in the mid-1960s. This led to a trade to the Baltimore Orioles in 1966 in one of the more lopsided deals in baseball history.

Robinson led the Orioles to the 1966 American League pennant, and a surprising upset of a powerful Los Angeles Dodger team in the World Series. Robinson that season won the Triple Crown and his second MVP award with a .316 batting average, 49 home runs and 122 RBI. He became the first player in baseball history to win MVP awards in both leagues.

He was the cornerstone of a late 1960s Orioles team that was dubbed "the best damn team in baseball" by Orioles manager Earl Weaver. They were,

winning three consecutive American League pennants and beating the Cincinnati Reds in the 1971 World Series in five games, surely a sweet win for Robinson.

In 1975, Robinson became the player-manager of the Cleveland Indians, the first black man to be a big league manager. In 1976, Robinson led the Indians to their first winning record (81-78) since 1968 and only their third winning record in 26 years. He would eventually manage the Indians, Giants and Orioles in an 11-year managing career.

LIFETIME STATS: BA: .294, HR: 586, RBI: 1,812, H: 2,943, SB: 204.

14. Edwin Lee "Eddie" Mathews, 3B-1B-OF, Braves, Astros, Tigers, 1952–68. Hall of Fame, 1978.

No less an authority than Ty Cobb once remarked that Eddie Mathews's swing was the most perfect he had ever seen.

Mathews was the best third baseman of his era, a powerful, agile man with a cannon for an arm and tremendous pop in his bat. His 486 home runs as a third baseman (he has 512 overall) was a record until Mike Schmidt broke it.

Mathews was one of the best high school baseball players of any era, and he signed with the Boston Braves on the night of his high school graduation in 1949. He only spent a couple of years in the minors before being brought up to Boston in 1952.

Mathews played well in 1952, but in 1953, he blossomed. He had one of the best seasons a 21-year-old player ever had, hitting .302 with 135 RBI and a league-leading 47 home runs.

Mathews's improvement coincided with the ascension of the Braves. After several moribund decades in Boston, the Braves moved out to the

Midwest. They were embraced by the city of Milwaukee, and were strong pennant contenders throughout the 1950s, reaching the World Series in 1957 and 1958.

Mathews, along with Hank Aaron, Lew Burdette and other stars, was one of the keys of the team. After losing a heartbreaking pennant race to the Dodgers in 1956, the Braves came back in 1957 and won the world championship over the Yankees in a stirring seven-game Series.

Mathews was one of the stars of the Series. His 10th-inning home run off Bob Grim won Game Four, and his backhanded grab of a Bill Skowron line drive in Game Seven was the final out of the Series. He only hit .227 in the seven-game matchup, but four of his hits were for extra bases.

Mathews was still a fixture at third base for Milwaukee into the mid-1960s, but his power numbers declined after 1961. In 1966, the Braves moved from Milwaukee to Atlanta, making Mathews the only player to play in three cities with one franchise.

LIFETIME STATS: BA: .271, HR: 512, RBI: 1,453, H: 2,315, SB: 68.

15. Carl Michael "Yaz" Yastrzemski, OF-1B-DH, Red Sox, 1961–83. Hall of Fame, 1989.

Yastrzemski did everything well, and he did it well for a long time. The 5'11" Yastrzemski was a baseball and basketball stand-out from Long Island who signed with Notre Dame to do both, but left the university when he signed a baseball contract after his freshman year.

Yaz was being groomed to be Ted Williams's replacement in left field, a hefty load for anyone's shoulders. And when Williams retired after the 1960 season, Yastrzemski moved right into his left field slot. He didn't overpower anyone in 1961, hitting .266 with 11 home runs, 80 RBI and 155 hits. But he did lead the team in total bases with 231 and extra base hits with 48.

Yastrzemski improved considerably in 1962, hitting .296 with 19 homers, 191 hits and 94 RBI. And in 1963, Yaz arrived, winning his first batting title with a .321 average and leading the league in hits with 183 and an on-base percentage of .418.

By the 1963 season, Yastrzemski was a fixture in left field. And the Red Sox, mired in mediocrity, were beginning to climb back toward respectability over the next few seasons.

In 1967, Yastrzemski put it all together, winning the Triple Crown with a .326 batting average, 44 home runs and 121 RBI, which also earned him an MVP award. Not coincidentally, the Red Sox also put it all together, winning their first American League championship since 1948. Boston lost a thrilling seven-game World Series to the St. Louis Cardinals, but Yastrzemski hit .400 with three home runs to lead the Sox. The 1967 season remains the most exciting season in Red Sox history, and one of the most exciting in baseball history.

With all his offensive numbers, it is easy to overlook the fact that Yastrzemski was also a great defensive player. He won seven Gold Gloves over his career, and led American League outfielders in assists in 1962, 1963, 1964 and 1966. He owned the Green Monster, which is the term Boston fans use for the left-field wall in Fenway Park. Yastrzemski knew every rivet, every dent and every nuance of the Wall, and his presence in left was a huge advantage for Boston.

In 1979, Yastrzemski became the first American League player to make 400 home runs and 3,000 hits. Three other players, Hank Aaron, Willie Mays and Stan Musial did it in the National League.

LIFETIME STATS: BA: .285, HR: 452, RBI: 1,844, H: 3,419, SB: 168.

Clemens is one of best-conditioned athletes in baseball, and has been so since his days in Boston. It's all paying off, as he enters his 21st year as a starting pitcher.

Clemens was a legend in Boston for most of his 13 years there. He won three Cy Young awards with the Red Sox, in 1986, 1987 and 1991.

That 1986 season was one of the best seasons any pitcher has ever had. Clemens went a league-leading 24-4 with 238 strikeouts and a league-best 2.48 ERA. Early in the year, he set an American League record by striking out 20 Seattle Mariners. He won the regular season MVP and the All Star MVP that year as the Red Sox won the American League championship.

Clemens proved that 1986 was not a fluke, leading the league in wins (20), winning percentage (.690), complete games (18) and shutouts (7) in 1987 to win his second Cy Young.

Clemens was the best pitcher in the league from 1986 to 1991. That 1991 season was the year he won his third Cy Young award for Boston, leading the league in strikeouts, ERA and innings pitched.

In all, Clemens has won six ERA titles. Only Lefty Grove, with nine, has more. He has led the league in strikeouts five times, in shutouts six times and complete games three times.

From 1993 to 1996, Clemens battled injuries, and the Red Sox allowed him to sign with the Blue Jays. He bounced back emphatically, winning two more Cy Young awards in that city. In 1996, 10 years after he struck out 20 batters with Boston, Clemens repeated the feat with Toronto.

In 1999, he signed with the Yankees, and helped New York to a pair of world championships in 1999 and 2000. In 2001, at age 39, Clemens won yet another Cy Young award. In 2003, he won his 300th game. If the ageless Clemens ever retires, he is a first-ballot Hall of Famer.

LIFETIME STATS: W: 310, L: 166 Sv: 0, ERA: 3.19, SO: 4,099, CG: 117.

Spahn was the winningest left-handed pitcher of all time, and one of the greatest hurlers, left-handed or right-handed, in baseball history.

Because of his military service in World War II, Spahn didn't really get a chance to show his stuff until 1946. He had a brief stint with the Braves in 1942, but didn't come away with any decisions that year.

But when he returned from the war, "Spahnie," as some of his teammates called him, began to display the kind of pitching that would make him a star in the late 1940s and throughout the 1950s. He went only 8-5, but his 2.94 ERA led the team.

By 1947, Spahn went 21-10, the first of a major league record-tying 13 seasons with 20 or more wins. Eight times he would lead the National League in wins, including five years in a row, from 1957 to 1961. His 63 shutouts place him sixth all-time in the National League record books.

He was the mainstay of a Braves staff that, most years, wasn't very deep. In the late 1940s, Boston fans rested their hopes on Spahn and fellow pitcher Johnny Sain most years. It was, as most Braves fans knew, "Spahn and Sain and pray for rain."

Spahn began his career as a fastball pitcher who also could throw his curve for strikes. And from 1949 to 1952, he led the league in strike-outs. But as he got older, Spahn got smarter. He added a screwball and a slider, and he was the best of his generation in changing speeds on all those pitches.

In 1960, at the age of 39, Spahn pitched his first no-hitter. The next season, five days past his 40th birthday, he pitched his second.

The Braves won the National League crown in 1957 and again in 1958, and Spahn was at the top of his game. He won the Cy Young award in 1957, with a league-leading 21 wins, as well as 111 strikeouts and a 2.69 ERA. In 1958, he might have been even better, with 22 wins, a .667 winning percentage, 23 complete games and 290 innings pitched, all tops in the National League.

Spahn began to slow down in the early 1960s, and the Braves sold him to the Mets in 1965. He spent part of his season in New York and later was shipped to the Giants. He was released after the season, but continued to pitch in the minors for two more years before retiring at age 46.

LIFETIME STATS: W: 363, L: 245, Sv: 29, ERA: 3.09, SO: 2,583, CG: 382.

18. Lawrence Peter "Yogi" Berra, C-OF, Yankees, 1946–65. Hall of Fame, 1972.

Maybe it's because he doesn't look like a great athlete. Maybe it's because of all those odd sayings he is credited with uttering. But there are still baseball fans who are reluctant to regard Berra as the greatest catcher in baseball history. He is.

The hitting speaks for itself. Berra hit 10 or more home runs 16 years in a row, and 20 or more home runs 11 times, including 10 years in a row. He hit over .300 four times. He had over 90 RBI nine times. He hit 20 or more doubles eight times. In short, Berra's offensive prowess gave the Yankees a huge advantage over just about every other team in baseball in the 1950s.

Between 1949 and 1955, Berra led the Yankees in RBI every season and won MVP awards in 1951, 1954 and 1955.

He was, by far, the best bad-ball hitter ever in the American League. Berra's hand-eye coordination enabled him to golf low pitches right out of the ballpark, or slash at eyebrow-high offerings for base hits. And, according to most of the ballplayers who played with and against him, Berra was the toughest out in the last three innings in baseball for most of his career.

Yet for all that aggression at the plate, Berra was very tough to strike out. He never whiffed more than 38 times in a season, and averaged only 22 strikeouts per year.

But he was also an excellent fielder. He became one of four catchers to record a 1.000 fielding average in a season when he did it in 1958. He led the league in games caught and chances accepted by a catcher eight times, and led the league in double plays six times

Finally, Berra was an excellent handler of pitchers. That is said of most great catchers, but that's the point. Yogi was a great catcher. He caught Allie Reynolds's two no-hitters in 1949 and, of course, also caught Don Larsen's perfect game in the 1956 World Series.

LIFETIME STATS: BA: .285, HR: 358, RBI: 1,430, H: 2,150, SB: 30.

19. George Thomas "Tom Terrific" Seaver, RHP, Mets, Reds, White Sox, Red Sox, 1967–1986. Hall of Fame, 1991.

Seaver is fondly recalled by Mets fans as the first true star the franchise ever had.

Seaver was a star at the University of Southern California when he signed a contract with the Braves for $40,000. The contract was voided on a technicality, so the NCAA and baseball commissioner William Eckert offered Seaver's services to any team who would match the Braves' offer. The Phillies, Indians and Mets did so, and the names of all three teams were placed in a hat in the commissioner's office. The Mets won when Eckert pulled their name out of the hat.

The whole thing obviously paid off handsomely. A year after the drawing, Seaver went 16-13 for a truly horrible Mets team that finished last, 40$\frac{1}{2}$ games behind St. Louis. Not surprisingly, Seaver made the All Star team.

Seaver went 16-12 for another bad Mets team the next season and had his breakout year in 1969, going 25-7 and winning the Cy Young award. The Mets, of course, won the World Series over the Orioles.

Baseball historian Bill James suggests that, given Seaver's amazingly consistent performance with teams that, for the most part, didn't score a lot of runs for him, he may have been the greatest pitcher of all time. It's not an unreasonable point. Seaver was good when his teams were bad, and when he had a little help in terms of better run production and more consistent relief, he was very, very good. He won three Cy Young awards, in 1969, 1973 and 1975, won 20 or more games five times and led the league in wins three times.

He was the consummate professional, a fanatic about conditioning and a perfectionist on the field. He fired three one-hitters and one no-hitter. That came on June 16, 1968, shutting down the Cardinals. Seaver won his 300th game with the White Sox in 1984, firing a complete game, six-hitter to beat the Yankees, 4–1.

LIFETIME STATS: W: 311, L: 205, Sv: 1, ERA: 2.86, SO: 3,640, CG: 231.

20. Roy "Campy" Campenella, C-3B-OF, Baltimore Elite Giants (Negro Leagues), Brooklyn Dodgers, 1937–57. Hall of Fame, 1969.

Campenella would rate much higher had his career not been shortened by an auto accident in 1958 that paralyzed him. Does he move ahead of Berra? Possibly. But that's all speculation.

Campenella's 20-year pro career began when he signed a contract to play with the Baltimore Elite Giants at age 15. He learned from one of the all-time greats: catcher Biz Mackey. He played behind Mackey for several years, but by 1941, Campenella was an all star, hitting .344 and inviting comparisons to Josh Gibson.

Campenella was a star in the Negro Leagues, and major league owners salivated at the chance of getting him. He eventually signed with the Dodgers, and was an All Star eight years in a row, from 1949 to 1956.

He was a great player, strong, yet surprisingly agile. He hit .300 or better three times, 20 or more home runs seven times, and won three MVP awards, in 1951, 1953 and 1955. From 1949 to 1956, the Dodgers won five National League pennants and defeated the New York Yankees in a memorable seven-game World Series in 1955. In that Series, Campenella hit .259 with three doubles and two home runs.

Campenella was a durable player, but like most catchers, he endured nagging injuries throughout his career, which, at times, affected his production at the plate. But he rarely begged off in a game, catching more than 100 contests for the Dodgers every season but his first.

Campenella's 242 lifetime home runs were a record for a catcher at the time of his retirement in 1957, and he would have surely added to that total had he not been injured. But although he was in a wheelchair the rest of his life, Campanella spent most of the rest of his life working in community relations for the Dodgers until his death in 1993.

LIFETIME STATS: BA: 276, HR: 242, RBI: 865, H: 1,161, SB: 25.

21. George Howard Brett, 3B-DH, Royals, 1973–93. Hall of Fame, 1999.

Hard work and a laser-like focus were the principal reasons George Brett became one of the greatest third basemen of all time.

Brett did not set the world on fire his first couple of years with the Royals. In his first full season, he hit two home runs and managed only 47 RBI. But Brett listened to his pitching coach, Charlie Lau, who taught him to wait on pitches and hit to all fields. In his second full season, 1975, Brett batted .308 and led the league with 13 triples and 195 hits.

In 1976, Brett led the league with 215 hits and 14 triples and earned his first batting championship with a .333 average. He became, over the next decade and a half, one of the most consistent players in the game.

From 1975 to 1990, Brett hit over .300 11 times. Three other times, he hit .290 or better. He had more than 100 RBI four times in that span and scored more than 100 runs four times as well.

In 1979, Brett became the sixth player in major league history to hit 20 or more doubles, triples and home runs in the same year. He also hit .329 and led the league in hits with 212.

But his best year was 1980, when he won the MVP award. Brett flirted with .400 through most of the season, and ended up hitting .390. He also had a 37-game hitting streak and led the league with a .664 on-base percentage. Ironically, it was a year in which Brett battled various nagging injuries all season, and ended up playing in only 117 games.

Brett was not a one-dimensional guy, though. He won a Gold Glove in 1985 for his play at third base, and was one of the more fundamentally sound defensive players of his era.

In 1987, after 14 years at third base, Brett was switched to first base to make way for rookie Kevin Seitzer. He made the transition work, hitting .290 with 22 homers that season. In 1990, at age 37, Brett won his final batting title, hitting .329 with a league-leading 45 doubles.

LIFETIME STATS: BA: .305, HR: 317, RBI: 1,595, H: 3,154, SB: 201.

22. Johnny Lee Bench, C-3B, Reds, 1967–83. Hall of Fame, 1989.

The greatest catcher in National League history, Bench was a certified star almost as soon as he donned a catcher's mask for the Cincinnati Reds in 1967. At 18, after being named the MVP of the Carolina League, his uniform number was retired. A year later, he was playing in the major leagues, and by 1968, Bench was an All Star, hitting .275, with 15 home runs and 82 RBI. He set a rookie record by catching in 154 games, as well as hitting 40 doubles.

Bench was clearly a star, and he dominated the catcher's position for the next 15 years. He batted either fourth or fifth for the Cincinnati "Big Red Machine" of the late 1960s and early 1970s.

He was a fearful weapon for the Reds, hitting 20 or more home runs 11 times in his career, driving in 100 or more runs six times and hitting 30 or more doubles five times. He had very good power for a catcher, hitting 45 home runs in 1970, a record for a catcher, and driving in 148 runs that same year, which was also a record for that position.

Bench was an MVP in 1970 and again in 1972, but those seasons were only marginally better than most of his career: He was always a very good player, consistent and productive.

That kind of production alone would have made Bench a star. But he was also, by far, the best defensive catcher in the National League for a large part of his career. He won 10 consecutive Gold Glove awards, from 1968 to 1977, and set a National League record by catching in at least 100 games in his first 13 full seasons. He had a tremendous throwing arm, among the best of all time.

Bench played in four World Series, hitting .279 with five home runs and 14 RBI. He also hit .370 in 12 All Star games.

LIFETIME STATS: BA: .267, HR: 389, RBI: 1,376, H: 2,048, SB: 68.

23. Sanford "Sandy" Koufax, LHP, Dodgers, 1955–66. Hall of Fame, 1972.

Koufax may not have possessed, technically speaking, the fastest fastball in major league history. But as countless former opponents would swear, it was the liveliest—a ball that rivaled the legendary heater of Jack Armstrong, the comic-strip all-American. A ball, which, like Armstrong's, dropped down and then rose up on a batter in the same path to the plate, like a ping-pong ball in a wind tunnel.

Koufax was a slow starter as a big leaguer. He was a rookie on the 1955 Brooklyn World Series champs, cobbling together a 2-2 mark with a 3.02 ERA. But in his first major league start on Aug. 27 against the Reds, he struck out 14 in a 7–0 win. Clearly, he had something.

But there were also afternoons when Koufax didn't have it. In his first two years with the Dodgers, he was 4-6, striking out 60 and walking 57.

He became a regular in 1958, after the Dodgers moved to Los Angeles. In the more spacious confines of Dodger Stadium, Koufax felt he had a little more room for error. He was 11-11, with 131 strikeouts. Hitters batted a league low .223 against him.

As he cut down on his walks, Koufax got better and better. He added a sweeping curve ball to go with the fastball. In 1961, he was 18-13 and led the league in strikeouts with 269. Koufax would lead the National League in strikeouts four times, including an amazing year in which he struck out 382 men, a league record, in only 335 innings.

In 1962, he pitched his first no-hitter. He would follow it up with a no-hitter every year until 1965. That final no-hitter was also a perfect game against the Cubs on September 7. He led the league in ERA five consecutive years, from 1962 to 1966. He won Cy Young awards in 1963, 1965 and 1966. Not coincidentally, those were also years in which the Dodgers won the National League crown.

In 1965, he won Game Five of the World Series against the Minnesota Twins on a four-hit shutout. He then came back three days later to win the Series by throwing a three-hit shutout.

Koufax retired after the 1966 season, nursing various arm troubles. But five years later, he became the youngest man ever to be elected to the Hall of Fame at age 36.

LIFETIME STATS: W: 165, L: 87, Sv: 9, ERA: 2.76, SO: 2,396, CG: 137.

24. Eddie Clarence Murray, Orioles, Dodgers, Mets, Indians, Angels, 1B-DH-3B, 1977–97. Hall of Fame, 2003.

Murray was a player who almost never had a bad year. And this was a guy who played for 21 seasons.

Murray had 110 or more hits and 20 or more doubles for 19 consecutive seasons. He hit 20 or more home runs in 16 seasons and had 90 or more RBI in 12 seasons. His 5,397 total bases are fifth all-time.

Murray never won a batting title, but hit over .300 seven times. In fact, Murray was such an overpowering hitter that he won the 1977 Rookie of the Year award as a designated hitter, the first player ever to accomplish that. He became a regular at first base the next season.

Murray won three Gold Gloves with the Orioles at first base, from 1982 to 1984. In 1981 and 1982, he led the league's first basemen in fielding percentage, a feat he accomplished again in 1989, his first year with the Dodgers.

Murray's low-key demeanor never seemed to bother a vast majority of his teammates, but fans and the Oriole ownership, specifically former owner Edward Bennett Williams, had a problem with it.

Ignoring Murray's amazing consistency, Williams was often critical of his first baseman's apparent lack of desire. Murray rarely endeared himself to the media, refusing to talk to the press for many years. The situation eventually became untenable, and Murray was eventually shipped to the Dodgers.

But after a slow start in 1989, Murray rebounded to hit a career-high .330 with Los Angeles. He was traded back to the east coast in 1992 and responded by hitting .285, with 27 homers and 100 RBI for the Mets in 1993.

In 1996, after a stint in Cleveland, Murray returned briefly to the Orioles for the second half of the season, and helped his old team to the American League playoffs. He hit .400 in the first round of the playoffs against the Indians.

LIFETIME STATS:
BA: .287, HR: 504, RBI: 1,917, H: 3,255, SB: 110.

25. Ernest "Mr. Cub" Banks, 1B-SS, Chicago, 1953–71. Hall of Fame, 1977.

The greatest player in Cubs' history, Ernie Banks was a consistent breath of fresh air for a franchise that didn't have a lot of good years in the 1950s or 1960s.

Banks was a terrific athlete who, initially, wasn't particularly interested in baseball. He was a football, track and basketball star in high school, and he enjoyed playing softball more than baseball as a youngster.

But in the early 1950s, baseball was where the money was. Banks played briefly in the Negro Leagues, which included a stint with the Kansas City Monarchs. But Jackie Robinson had broken the color line a few years prior, and the good black players were beginning to be snapped up by big league teams.

It wasn't long before the Cubs discovered Banks. He was signed by Chicago in 1953 and brought up to the majors immediately. He played 10 games at the end of the season and hit .314. The next season, he was a regular and by 1955, Banks was a star.

His sunny demeanor, and perpetual enthusiasm were legendary. When he would say, "It's a great day for baseball. Let's play two!" it was not an act. Banks had a fine appreciation for the game.

And he was a heck of a player. He started his career as the Cubs' shortstop, and won MVP awards in 1958 and 1959. He led the league in home runs in 1958 (47) and 1960 (41). In fact, from 1955 to 1960, nobody in the majors, including Mickey Mantle and Henry Aaron, hit more home runs.

Defensively, he led National League shortstops in fielding percentage three times, and won a Gold Glove in 1960. He was switched to first base in 1962, but handled that change pretty well, leading the league in fielding percentage at that position in 1969 and leading first basemen in assists five times.

Banks retired in 1971, and the next year he became the first Cub to have his number retired.

LIFETIME STATS: BA: .274, HR: 512, RBI: 1,636, H: 2,583, SB: 50.

26. Calvin Edwin "Cal," "Iron Man" Ripken Jr., SS-3B, 1981–2001.

The man who broke the "unbreakable" record, Ripken began his amazing streak in 1983 and didn't miss a game until 18 years later. He played in 2,632 consecutive games, smashing Lou Gehrig's record of 2,131. And, it's fair to point out, Ripken played a vast majority of those games at shortstop, which, defensively, is a tougher position to play than first base.

But let's not forget that the guy was also really good. He hit .300 or better five times in his career. He won the MVP award in 1983 and again in 1991. Twelve times in his career, Ripken belted 20 or more home runs, and he had 100 or more RBI four times.

On defense, Ripken won two Gold Gloves, in 1991 and 1992. In 1990, Ripken's .996 fielding average was the best for a shortstop in baseball history. In fact, Ripken's .990 fielding average in 1989 is fourth best all time and his .989 in 1995 is tied for eighth best all time. His career lifetime fielding average of .979 is fifth-best.

LIFETIME STATS: BA: .276, HR: 431, RBI: 1,695, H: 3,184, SB: 36.

27. Edward Charles "Whitey," "The Chairman of the Board," "Slick" Ford, LHP, Yankees, 1950–67. Hall of Fame, 1974.

Whitey Ford pitched with a confident efficiency that made him one of the best "Big Game" pitchers in baseball history.

True, he played for a Yankee franchise that won 11 American League pennants and six World Championships in his tenure, but Ford's forte was taking the ball in big games and winning those games. Easier said than done.

He remains the leader in World Series wins with 10, games started with 22, as well as innings pitched, strikeouts and losses. Over the span of the 1961, 1962 and 1963 World Series, he pitched 33 consecutive shutout innings, breaking Babe Ruth's record of 29 2/3 innings with the Red Sox.

Ford's ERA during the regular season with New York was under 3.00 a total of 11 times, and he was the league leader twice, in 1956 and 1958. In 1961, he went 25-4 with 209 strikeouts to win the Cy Young award.

Ford only won 20 or more games twice in his career, but was a player unimpressed by stats anyway. Winning was the stat he cared more about.

LIFETIME STATS: W: 236, L: 106, Sv: 10, ERA: 2.75, SO: 1,956, CG: 156.

28. Edwin Donald "Duke," "The Silver Fox" Snider, OF, Dodgers, Mets, Giants, 1947–64. Hall of Fame, 1980.

Looking back, Duke Snider was probably considered the third-best of the three stellar center fielders who played in New York, after the Giants'

Willie Mays and the Yankees' Mickey Mantle. But Dodger fans of the day will gladly point out that the Duke of Flatbush, as he was called, hit more home runs than Mays or Mantle in the four years (1954-57) that all three men were manning center field in the Big Apple for their respective teams.

Snider was a part-time player for the first two years of his existence as a Dodger, but apt tutoring by George Sisler enabled Snider to adjust his stance slightly to better enable him to drive balls up and out of tiny Ebbets Field. He hit 40 or more home runs five consecutive years, from 1953 to 1957, leading the league in 1956 with 43.

Snider was a strong defensive player, with a powerful throwing arm and excellent speed.

Snider was one of the best post-season players ever, setting National League records for home runs (11) and RBI (26). In the 1952 and again in the 1955 Fall Classic, Snider hit four home runs. He is the only man to do so twice in World Series history.

LIFETIME STATS: BA: .295, HR: 407, RBI: 1,333, H: 2,116, SB: 99.

29. Steven Norman "Steve," "Lefty" Carlton, LHP, Cardinals, Phillies, Giants, White Sox, Indians, Twins, 1965–88. Hall of Fame, 1994.

Carlton is the number–two left-hander of all time, in terms of wins, behind Warren Spahn, and the number–two all-time in strikeouts, behind Nolan Ryan.

Interestingly, when Carlton first began trying out for big league teams, there was some question as to his arm strength. In response, Carlton became almost a fitness fanatic, and within a few years was one of the hardest throwers in the game.

He became a solid, dependable starter with the Cardinals in 1967 to 1968, going 27-20 as St. Louis won back-to-back National League pennants. But his persistent salary demands were wearing out the Cardinal front office, and he was traded to the Phillies.

That trade was the turning point in Carlton's career. He became an instant star in Philadelphia, winning the Cy Young award four times while there: in 1972, 1977, 1980 and 1982. Carlton was the first pitcher to win four awards, although he has since been eclipsed by Roger Clemens, who has six.

That first Cy Young might have been the best. Carlton won 27 games for a team that won only 59 total. He led the league in complete games, (30), innings pitched (346 1/3) and strikeouts (310), becoming only the second National League pitcher to amass more than 300 strikeouts in a season. (Sandy Koufax was the first.)

Carlton developed a devastating slider to go with his fastball and won the strikeout crown five times in all.

LIFETIME STATS: W: 329, L: 244, Sv: 2, ERA: 3.22, SO: 4,136, CG: 254.

30. Walter Fenner "Buck" Leonard, 1B-OF, Homestead Grays (Negro Leagues), 1934-50. Hall of Fame, 1972.

Leonard was a left-handed pull hitter who was the anchor for the legendary Homestead Grays in the 1930s and 1940s.

He was born in North Carolina, the oldest of six children. His parents called him "Buddy," but one of his younger brothers couldn't pronounce that name very well, instead calling his older sibling "Buck." The name stuck.

Leonard began his pro career playing in semi-pro Negro Leagues in North Carolina. But his fearsome hitting drew the attention of Cumberland "Cum" Posey, the manager-owner of the Grays. Leonard signed a contract to play for the Grays in the summer of 1933. For the next 17 years, he was the team's starting first baseman.

Leonard was a very good hitter, recording team-leading batting averages of .356 in 1936, .396 in 1937, .397 in 1938, .394 in 1939 and .378 in 1940, as the Grays won the Negro National League five consecutive years. His .397 in 1938 also led the Negro National League.

In 1942, when catcher Josh Gibson joined Leonard and the Grays, the two men became known as the "Thunder Twins," and led the Homesteads to three more NL titles, and Negro League World Series championships in 1943 and 1944.

Leonard was a solid defensive first baseman, described by observers at the time as being as agile as the legendary Hal Chase.

LIFETIME STATS: BA: .335, H: 779, HR: 79.

31. Louis Clark "Lou" Brock, OF, Cubs, Cardinals, 1961–79. Hall of Fame, 1985.

Brock was a weak-hitting but explosively fast outfielder with the Cubs when, in 1964, he was traded to the St. Louis Cardinals for pitcher Ernie Broglio. Broglio was a decent pitcher, but at the time, Brock was deemed a lousy outfielder. The conventional wisdom of the time was the Cardinals got snookered.

They didn't. The trade galvanized Brock. He hit .348 with 33 stolen bases and 81 runs scored in 103 games for the Cardinals as St. Louis surged to the pennant and beat the Yankees in a stirring seven-game World Series. It is regarded as one of the worst trades ever, possibly the worst ever in the National League, and not far from the Ruth trade.

Brock went on to become a feared leadoff hitter, even though his strikeouts were exceptionally high for a leadoff man. Still, he led the league in stolen bases eight times, including a National League record 118 in 1974, when Brock was 35.

He was sensational in the postseason, hitting .391

in three World Series, which is second all-time for players who played in two or more Fall Classics. In the 1967 and the 1968 Series, Brock hit over .400 both times.

LIFETIME STATS: BA: .293, HR: 149, RBI: 900, H: 3,023, SB: 938.

32. Reginald Martinez "Reggie," "Mr. October" Jackson, OF-DH, Athletics, Orioles, Yankees, Angels, 1967–87. Hall of Fame, 1993.

Jackson's outspoken behavior sometimes (well, actually most of the time) overshadowed a prodigious talent. He remains one of the better "big game" players in the history of the game.

Jackson played on 10 divisional championship teams, six pennant winners and five World Champions. Jackson's batting average in five World Series is .357, almost 100 points better than his career average. His career World Series slugging average of .755 is still a record.

In 1977, he hit three home runs in the deciding game of the World Series, off three different pitchers on three consecutive pitches, perhaps one of the most dramatic performances in World Series history.

He wasn't a slouch during the regular season, either. Jackson was MVP in 1973, when he led the American League in home runs (32), runs scored (99), RBI (117) and slugging percentage (.531). He led the league in round-trippers four times, in 1973, 1975, 1980 and 1982.

Jackson could also run the bases, stealing 20 or more four times in his career and averaging about 24 doubles per year for his career.

He struck out an awful lot, though, and his 2,597 whiffs are still the most ever.

He also had a big mouth. In 1977, when he was acquired by New York, he told a writer he was "the straw that stirred the drink", which alienated team-mate Thurman Munson and manager Billy Martin. He was, but there was no reason to trumpet the fact. Basically, Jackson's philosophy was: It ain't bragging if you can do it. And he could.

LIFETIME STATS: BA: .262, HR: 563, RBI: 1,702, H: 2,584, SB: 228.

33. Roberto Walker "Arriba" Clemente, OF, Pirates, 1955–72. Hall of Fame, 1973.

Clemente was an outstanding defensive outfielder who was also one of the most consistent hitters of the 1950s and 1960s.

Clemente was noted more for his defensive abilities in the early part of his career. He had a strong, accurate throwing arm from the outfield, and his speed and athleticism enabled him to track down balls that would have eluded most defenders. He would go on to win 12 Gold Glove awards for his fielding and lead National League outfielders in assists five times.

Gradually, Clemente's offensive abilities began to catch up with his defensive prowess, but it wasn't until he won the first of four batting titles in 1961 (with a .351 average) that people began noticing that facet of his game.

In the 1960s, Roberto Clemente became a bona fide star, winning three more batting championships in 1964, 1965 and 1967, and the MVP award in 1966. Gradually, the Pirates were getting better, too.

Clemente's showcase came in the 1971 World Series. He had played well in the 1960 Fall Classic with Pittsburgh, hitting .310 as the Pirates upset the Yankees. But in 1971, Clemente was amazing, hitting .414 and slugging .759 to become MVP of the Series as the Pirates defeated the Orioles in seven games.

On New Year's Eve, 1972, Clemente was on board a plane flying to Managua, Nicaragua with relief supplies for earthquake victims there. His plane encountered turbulence, and crashed about a mile off the Puerto Rican coast. There were no survivors. The five-year waiting period for induction into the Hall of Fame was waived and Clemente was immediately inducted.

LIFETIME STATS: BA: .317, HR: 240, RBI: 1,305, H: 3,000, SB: 83.

34. Robin R. Yount, SS-OF, 1974–93, Brewers. Hall of Fame, 1999.

Yount was only 18 when he started for the Brewers at shortstop in 1974. He learned quickly, cracking 28 doubles and 149 hits his second year in the bigs. By 1980, Yount was a star, leading the league with 49 doubles and 82 extra-base hits.

An aggressive weight-training regimen paid off in 1982, when his power numbers jumped. Yount hit 29 homers, 12 triples, a league-leading 46 doubles and scored 129 runs to earn the MVP award as the Brewers won the American League championship that year. Yount hit .414 in his only World Series appearance, a loss to the St. Louis Cardinals.

A shoulder injury forced the Brewers to move Yount to the outfield. He adapted well, hitting over .300 from 1986 to 1989. He won his second MVP award in 1989, hitting .318 with 195 hits, 21 home runs, 38 doubles and nine triples.

Yount was not particularly fast, but he was a smart base runner, stealing 15 or more bases nine times in his career.

Yount got his 3,000th hit at age 37, one of the youngest players ever to accomplish that feat.

LIFETIME STATS: BA: .285, HR: 251, RBI: 1,406, H: 3,142, SB: 271.

35. Anthony Keith "Tony" Gwynn, OF-DH, Padres, 1982–2000.

Gwynn parlayed a tremendous work ethic into becoming one of the great National League hitters of modern times. And he was no slouch in the outfield, either.

Gwynn was a third-round pick by the Padres in 1981, and came up to the big club a year later. He was also a first round pick of the NBA's San Diego Clippers. Gwynn hit .289 in limited action with San Diego, but his work ethic impressed his coaches.

In 1984, he became the first Padre to make more than 200 hits (he had 213) as well as the first San Diego player to win a batting title, with a .351 average. It was the first of eight batting titles for Gwynn. Only Ty Cobb has more crowns.

For several seasons in the late 1980s and early 1990s, Gwynn would get off to an explosive start, and sportswriters would speculate about his chances of hitting .400. Gwynn never made it, but in 1994, his .394 average was the best in the National League since Bill Terry's .401 in 1930. It was the first of four consecutive batting championships for Gwynn.

Never much of a power hitter, Gwynn was an excellent base runner. He hit 21 or more doubles 16 consecutive years, and tied a record in 1986 with five stolen bases in one game. In 1987, he stole 56 bases, good for second in the league.

Originally a fair to poor fielder, Gwynn's work ethic eventually earned him five Gold Gloves in the outfield.

LIFETIME STATS:
BA: .338, HR: 134, RBI: 1,121, H: 3,108, SB: 318.

36. Charles Leo "Gabby" Hartnett, C, Cubs, Giants, 1922–41. Hall of Fame, 1955.

As a first-year player with the Cubs in 1922, Hartnett was shy around his new teammates, which led to his ironic nickname. But until Johnny Bench came along, Hartnett was considered the best catcher in the history of the National League.

His strength was fielding, and he led National League catchers in fielding percentage six times in his career, including a record-tying four consecutive times from 1934 to 1937. Hartnett also led the league in assists six times, in putouts four times and in double plays six times.

But Hartnett's most famous moment came while at bat. On Sept. 28, 1938, Hartnett was at bat against the Pirates in the bottom of the ninth, with the score 5–5 and two strikes on him. Hartnett had taken over management of the team at mid-season, and the Cubs were charging toward a pennant, trailing Pittsburgh by a half-game at that point.

As darkness began to fall, Hartnett slammed a game-winning home run to put his team in first place. Three games later, the Cubs were National League champs, and the "Homer in the Gloamin' " was a part of baseball lore.

Hartnett was actually a pretty good hitter, so the home run was not a complete surprise. He hit .300 or better six times in his career, and won the MVP award in 1930 with a .339 batting average, 37 home runs and 122 RBI. The latter two stats were career highs.

LIFETIME STATS: BA: .297, HR: 236, RBI: 1,179, H: 1,912, SB: 28.

37. Harmon Clayton "Killer," "The Fat Kid" Killebrew, 1B-3B-OF-DH, Senators, Twins, Royals, 1954–75. Hall of Fame, 1984.

A tremendous power hitter, Harmon Killebrew played several positions the Senators and Twins over his career, and always seemed to handle them pretty well. His forte was obviously at the plate, but Killebrew was fundamentally sound enough to play well wherever he had to.

He actually didn't become a starter until his sixth year in the majors, and only then after an injury to infielder Pete Runnels. But that season, the Killer bashed 42 home runs to lead the league, the first of eight years he would hit 40 or more dingers.

His power was awesome. In 1962, he hit a ball completely out of vast Tiger Stadium. In 1967, his three-run blast shattered two seats in the upper deck of Minnesota's Metropolitan Stadium. The seats were painted orange and never sold again.

Killebrew, for a while, seemed poised to break some of Babe Ruth's home run records in the mid-1960s. But the muscular Minnesotan began suffering nagging injuries that usually didn't sit him down, but did hamper his production.

Killebrew had his best season in 1969, and won the MVP award while hitting 49 home runs, with a 140 RBI, 145 walks and a .430 slugging percentage, all league bests. He also had 153 hits and stole a career-high eight bases.

He probably should have ended his career in Minnesota, but after a contract squabble, Killebrew found himself in Kansas City in 1975.

LIFETIME STATS:
BA: .256, HR: 573, RBI: 1,584, H: 2,086, SB: 19.

38. Pack Robert "Bob," "Hoot" Gibson, RHP, Cardinals, 1959–75. Hall of Fame, 1981.

One of the best "money" pitchers ever, Gibson combined a fierce competitiveness with tremendous athleticism to become one of the premiere pitchers of the 1960s.

Gibson was a great pitcher in the regular season: He won 20 or more games five times in his career, and seven times he completed 20 or more games in a season.

But his World Series pitching was even more impressive. He won seven World Series games in a row, and those seven career victories are second only to the Yankees' Whitey Ford. His World Series ERA is a miniscule 1.89 and he completed eight of his nine starts.

In 1968, he set a World Series record with 17 strikeouts in Game One of the series. He won the seventh game in both the 1964 and 1967 World Series.

Gibson's 1968 season was one of the greatest seasons of all time. He went 22-9, with a league-leading 13 shutouts, completed 28 of his 34 starts, struck out a league-leading 268 batters and turned in an incredible 1.12 ERA, still the lowest of the 20th century for a pitcher throwing 300 innings or more. At one point, he allowed two runs in 92 innings. That effort earned him the Cy Young and Most Valuable Player awards. He would also win another Cy Young in 1970.

He was a great athlete, and fielded his position very well, earning nine Gold Gloves. A fierce competitor, he hated to come out of games. His catchers usually weren't too thrilled to visit him on the mound during games, either.

LIFETIME STATS: W: 251, L: 174, Sv: 6, ERA: 2.91, SO: 3,117, CG: 255.

Top 10 Pitchers (1900–1950)

1. Walter "The Big Train," "Barney" Johnson, RHP, Senators, 1907–27. Hall of Fame, 1936.

Johnson was a 6'1" strikeout machine, an affable soul who could buzz a baseball from the mound to home plate as fast as anyone in history.

It was, at least partly, the arms. Johnson had long, limber arms, and he threw the ball with an easy sidearm motion that arrived in his catcher's mitt with a sound like a rifle shot.

Johnson played his entire career with the Washington Senators, an organization not particularly known for its acumen. With Johnson leading the way, the Senators did manage a pair of World Series appearances, and in 1924, he was a world champion.

The story of that final game is one of the fine yarns of World Series play. Johnson pitched four innings of scoreless relief in Game Seven after pitching a complete game two days earlier. Teammate Early McNeely's 12th-inning seeing-eye single scored the winning run.

Johnson was the Sultan of Strikeouts, to borrow a nickname from his contemporary, Babe Ruth. The Big Train (so named for the locomotive-like velocity of his pitches), led the league in strikeouts 12 times, in shutouts seven times, in wins and complete games six times and in ERA five times.

Johnson won 417 games and saved 34 more for the Senators. He was as affable as Ty Cobb was rambunctious. Old-timers swore that when Johnson was far ahead in a game, he would ease up on a rookie or former teammate and let them get a hit. It's probably true.

LIFETIME STATS: W: 417, L: 279, Sv: 34, ERA: 2.17, SO: 3,509, CG: 531.

2. Robert Moses "Lefty" Grove, LHP, A's, Red Sox, 1925–41. Hall of Fame, 1947.

For most of his career, Lefty Grove was a surly SOB. He had a sizzling fastball and a temper to match it.

Maybe it was because the big left-hander didn't get a chance to pitch in the big leagues until he was 25. He starred for the Baltimore Orioles, then a minor league squad, in the early 1920s, helping them win several International League championships.

Grove was finally sold to the Philadelphia A's for $100,600 in 1920. That was more than the $100,000 fee the Yankees paid for Babe Ruth.

Grove was worth every penny–eventually. He was a tremendous pitcher as a rookie, leading the league in both strikeouts (116) and walks (131) in 1925. He ended up 10-12 that year, his only losing record in the major leagues.

By 1927, Grove was still blowing fastballs by hitters, and his placement was improving, as well. He struck out a league-high 174 batters and walked only 79. Grove would lead the league in strikeouts seven consecutive years while with Philadelphia.

In 1931, Grove went 31-4, with 27 complete games and four shutouts, both league highs. He also struck out a league-best 175 batters and won the ERA crown with a 2.06 mark. It was his best year.

Grove won nine ERA titles in his career. No other pitcher to date has won more than six.

For whatever reason, Grove didn't hesitate to brush back, or hit, batters. He often scowled at teammates who made a bad play behind him.

In 1934, Grove was traded to the Boston Red Sox, who hoped Lefty could anchor a staff that would win a World Series. That didn't happen, mostly because Grove sustained an injury to his left shoulder that dropped him to 8-8 that year.

But Grove was smart as well as talented. He was no longer a power pitcher, but he relied on guile and a good slider to win games now. He won 17 or more games three times with Boston, including a 20-12 mark in 1935.

Grove staggered to the finish line in 1941, going 7-7 and winning his 300th and last game. He retired to his home town of Lonaconing, Maryland, and opened a bowling alley.

LIFETIME STATS: W: 300, L: 141, Sv: 55, ERA: 3.06, SO: 2,266, CG: 298.

3. Grover Cleveland "Pete" Alexander, RHP, Phillies, Cubs, Cardinals, 1911–1930. Hall of Fame, 1938.

Grover Cleveland Alexander is remembered, when he is remembered at all, as the guy who pitched drunk in the 1926 World Series. It's an unfortunate distinction, because Alexander was one of the greatest pitchers in the history of the game.

He had an amazing rookie season, leading the league in wins (28), complete games (31) shutouts (seven) and innings pitched (367). Four of those shutouts were consecutive, including a 1–0 win over Cy Young, then in his final season.

He was a workhorse for the Phillies, leading them to the National League championship in 1915. That season, Alexander led the National League in wins (31), complete games (36), shutouts (12), innings pitched (376 1/3), strikeouts (241) and ERA (1.22).

That was a great year for "Old Pete," as he was called then, but it was about routine for Alexander, who led the league in wins, strikeouts and complete games six times each, shutouts and innings pitched seven times each and ERA five times. From 1915 to 1920, six years in a row, Alexander's ERA was below 2.00.

He did it with a rising fastball that he could throw at several different velocities, and a great, looping curve ball that he could throw for strikes at any point in the count. He almost never walked anyone and he usually pitched very well in big games.

That was why the St. Louis Cardinals picked him up in midseason in 1926. Alexander won nine games down the stretch for St. Louis, propelling the National Leaguers into the World Series against the powerful Yankees.

Alexander had pitched a masterful Game Six in Yankee Stadium that year, winning 10–2, and figured he wouldn't have to worry about appearing in Game Seven. Which is why he was in Billy LaHiff's tavern in Manhattan the night before that final game. He closed LaHiff's and missed batting practice the next afternoon.

In the bottom of the seventh, the Cardinals were ahead, 3–2, but the bases were loaded. So was Alexander, but he got future Hall-of-Famer Tony Lazzeri on knee-high fastballs to get him out and pitched two more scoreless innings for the win.

LIFETIME STATS: W: 373, L: 208, Sv: 32, ERA: 2.56, SO: 2,198, CG: 437.

4. Denton True "Cy" Young, RHP, Cleveland Spiders, Cardinals, Red Sox, Indians, Braves, 1890– 1911. Hall of Fame, 1937.

Cy Young not only set the world record for winning baseball games by the end of his amazing career, he truly sparked the evolution of baseball itself. When Young started, pitchers threw out of a box 50 feet from home plate. By the time he retired, pitchers stood on a mound 60 feet, six inches from the plate and fired the ball in.

Young was effective either way. He won 30 or more games five times in his career, and 10 other times won 20 or more. He led the league in wins five times, in shutouts seven times and in saves twice. He won more games (511), lost more (316), pitched more innings (7,354 2/3) and completed more games (749) than any pitcher, ever. He was durable, versatile and tough as nails.

His nickname was reportedly earned when he was being warmed up by a young catcher in his minor league days, and several of his pitches got past the young man and damaged a fence behind the fellow. The catcher remarked that the fence looked like a "cyclone" had hit it, and thus was born the tag.

Young became a canny veteran only two or three years into his professional career. He threw a fastball and curve, and he threw those pitches from various angles at various speeds. He also understood that many major league teams of the 19th century didn't like to use up too many balls during a game, as the balls cost money. So those balls tended to get softer and more lopsided as games went on. Young rarely asked an umpire for a new ball, because he could make lopsided or scuffed balls dance like an ant on a hot stove.

But Young's greatest secret was that he was as limber as an Indian yogi. He rarely warmed up by throwing more than a handful of pitches, and was usually ready to pitch again on a day's rest. This advantage appeared to be a natural one, as Young clearly wasn't an exercise buff, particularly at the end of his career. By 1911, Young had to retire, because at 44, he was so rotund that batters would bunt on him and make him field the ball.

No matter, Young was a great, great pitcher for many years, and he is now annually honored by the most valuable pitcher's award that carries his name. No one deserves it more.

LIFETIME STATS: W: 511, L: 316, Sv: 17, ERA: 2.63, SO: 2,803, CG: 749.

5. Robert William Andrew "Rapid Robert" Feller, RHP, Indians, 1936–-56. Hall of Fame, 1962.

Interestingly, although Bob Feller was clearly the fastest pitcher of his era, he always credited his numerous strikeout records to his curve ball and slider.

Feller was something of a prodigy when he got to the big leagues. He was signed by Cleveland as a 17-year-old and brought up to the big club immediately. In his major league debut against the St. Louis Browns near the end of the 1936 season, he struck out 15 batters. Later in the year, Feller struck out 17 men in a game against the A's.

Curveball and slider notwithstanding, it was Feller's fastball that was doing all the damage initially. Feller threw an extremely "live" ball, which meant that it jumped around as it neared the plate.

And with this velocity came a certain degree of wildness, at first. In 1937, Feller's first full year with Cleveland, he struck out 150 and walked 106. In 1938, the year he led the league in strikeouts with 240, he also walked 208, which was a major league record at the time.

But Feller was already learning to nick the edge of the plate with his fastball. The 1938 season was the first of seven years he would lead the league in strikeouts. He won 20 or more games six times, and also led the league in complete games six times.

Feller fired three no-hitters, including an opening day gem against the White Sox in 1940. Feller also threw 12 one-hitters.

Feller lost four years to World War II, but when he returned to baseball in 1946, he had clearly lost nothing off his fastball. His 348 strikeouts broke Rube Waddell's league record, and in 1948, he led the Indians to their first World Series championship in 28 years.

But after that season, the Feller fastball lost a little speed, and Rapid Robert became a little more canny on the mound. He had one more solid season in 1951, leading the league in wins with 22. But in his final five years with the Indians, Feller was 36-31. He was a very effective spot starter with the Indians in 1954, when Cleveland once again won the pennant, but didn't pitch in the World Series against the Giants.

LIFETIME STATS: W: 266, L: 162, Sv: 21, ERA: 3.25, SO: 2,581, CG: 279.

Mathewson was probably not the clean-cut golden

6. Christopher "Christy," "Big Six," "Matty" Mathewson, RHP, Giants, Reds, 1900–16. Hall of Fame, 1936.

boy that newsmen of the day made him seem, but he was probably pretty close. And his pitching abilities were certainly not exaggerated.

"Big Six" (named after a famous fire engine in New York City) was a masterful control pitcher who possessed pinpoint accuracy and could vary the speed of his fastball, curveball and change-up so well that he appeared to have six or seven different pitches to call on.

Mathewson also was one of the early masters of what was then called the "fadeaway" pitch, which modern players call a screwball, because it broke in on right-handed hitters. The whole package was impressive.

Mathewson started his career slowly, going 34-37 from 1900 to 1902. But the 1902 season record was misleading: although he was 14-17 that year, Mathewson led the league in shutouts with eight. In 1903, he turned the corner, going 30-13, and never won fewer than 22 games for the next 12 years.

From 1903 to 1905, Matty was awe-inspiring. He won 30, 33 and 31 games, with a total of 18 shutouts and 685 strikeouts. He averaged about 2 walks per nine innings in that span, and in fact was always a very, very good control pitcher.

Eleven times in his career, Mathewson pitched 300 innings or more in a season. In the 1908 season, when he won a career-high 37 games, he led the league with a miniscule 1.43 ERA to go along with 259 strikeouts and threw 390 2/3 innings. He started 44 games and completed 34, while also saving five games.

He was John McGraw's unofficial adopted son, and the McGraws and Mathewsons often spent time together in the off-season. In 1936, he was one of the five original players elected to the Hall of Fame.

LIFETIME STATS: W: 373, L: 188, Sv: 28, ERA: 2.13, SO: 2,502, CG: 434.

7. Carl Owen "King Carl," "The Meal Ticket" Hubbell, LHP, Giants, 1928–43. Hall of Fame, 1947.

The nicknames alone give you a hint of how good this guy was. Hubbell, an affable Oklahoman, won 20 games or more five years in a row for the Giants between 1933 and 1937. He was the National League MVP in both 1933 and 1936, the only non-wartime pitcher to do that in baseball history (Hal Newhouser did it with Detroit in 1944 and 1945).

Hubbell was a seven-time All Star, and the game for which he is best known was the 1934 All Star Game. After giving up a single to Charley Gehringer in the first inning, Hubbell then walked Heinie Manush. He then proceeded to strike out Babe Ruth (looking), Lou Gehrig (swinging) and Jimmie Foxx (swinging). He came back in the second inning and punched out Joe Cronin (swinging) and Al Simmons (swinging). That's five Hall-of-Famers in a row, which has got to be some kind of record.

Hubbell's left arm, by the end of his career, was twisted almost completely around by the action of throwing tens of thousands of screwballs.

LIFETIME STATS: W: 253, L: 154, Sv: 33, ERA: 2.98, SO: 1,677.

8. Joseph "Smokey Joe" Williams, RHP, Chicago Giants, New York Lincoln Giants, Chicago American Giants, Atlantic City Bacharach Giants, Hilldale Daisies, Homestead Grays, Detroit Wolves (Negro Leagues), 1905–32. Hall of Fame, 1999.

Williams, a lanky 6'4" fireballer from Texas, was the first real pitching star in the Negro Leagues. Armed with a hellacious fastball, Williams set all kinds of strikeout records for the various teams on which he played.

Williams had at least a dozen 20-strikeout games over his career, including a classic battle against the Kansas City Monarchs' Chet Brewer in 1930, when, as the starter for the Homestead Grays, William struck out 25 men in a 12-inning game in a 1–0 win. Brewer didn't do too bad either, striking out 19 men.

Prior to that, his most famous game was in 1917, when he no-hit the New York Giants of the National League in an exhibition game, although he lost the game 1–0 on an error. But it was reportedly that day that Giant star Ross Youngs dubbed Williams "Smokey Joe."

Williams reportedly had his best game against white major leaguers; his record against big-league clubs is 8-4. He also shut out the Giants in 1912, 6–0, on three hits, a few weeks after they lost the World Series to the Boston Red Sox, and, coincidentally, another "Smokey Joe," this pitcher being Boston's "Smokey Joe" Wood.

Wood was also an excellent batter, and at least twice hit better than .300 in a season.

LIFETIME STATS: W: 107, L: 57.

9. Jay Hanna "Dizzy" Dean, RHP, Cardinals, Cubs, 1930, 1932–41, 1947. Hall of Fame, 1953.

Dean was given his nickname by an unsympathetic sergeant in the U.S. Army, who had little patience for Private Dean's shenanigans. Dean came up to the Cardinals on the last day of the season in 1930 and tossed a complete-game three-hitter.

Despite that performance, Dean didn't get another chance with St. Louis until 1932, when he made the Opening Day roster. But he showed the Cardinals he was worth it, winning 18 games and leading the league in innings pitched, strikeouts and shutouts.

For the next four years, Dean was the best pitcher in baseball, by a country mile. He averaged 27 wins, 25 complete games, 311 innings pitched, 197 strike-outs, four shutouts, 50 starts and even seven saves a season over that span. Batters hit .252 against him and he walked a little fewer than two batters a game over that span. It is one of the most overpowering four-year stretches in baseball history.

In 1933, Dean struck out 17 batters in a game against the Cubs, a major league record at the time. Dean won the MVP award in 1934, and came in second the next two years.

In 1937, Dean, the starter for the National League in the All Star game, was hit in the foot by a line drive off the bat of Earl Averill. Dean sat out the first few weeks of the second half of the season but tried to come back too early. To compensate for his injured foot, Dean changed his delivery and suffered bursitis in his pitching arm.

The following year, Dean was traded to the Cubs, and became a spot starter, winning seven of eight games and helping Chicago to the National League pennant. But he would win only nine more games in his career.

LIFETIME STATS: W: 150, L: 83, Sv: 30, ERA: 3.02, SO: 1,163, CG: 154.

10. Mordecai Peter Centennial "Three-Finger," "Miner" Brown, RHP, Cardinals, Cubs, St. Louis (FL), Brooklyn (FL), Chicago Whales (FL), 1903–16. Hall of Fame, 1949.

Brown is the ultimate lemons-to-lemonade ballplayer. As a seven-year-old, he caught his right hand in his father's corn grinder. That cost him his forefinger, which was amputated. His middle finger was permanently mangled. His little finger was cut to a stub.

But Brown learned to pitch by spinning the ball off his twisted middle finger, which, coupled with the velocity with which Brown threw, gave it a twisting, darting motion that was difficult for hitters to pick up.

Brown was signed by the Cardinals and struggled to a 9-13 record. But Cub manager Frank Chance liked Brown's toughness, and got him for Chicago in 1904. It was a fortuitous pickup. For six seasons, from 1906 to 1911, Brown won 20 or more games. His ERA from 1904 to 1908 was under 2.00 four of those five years. He also wasn't afraid to pitch in relief between starts. He led the league in saves from 1908 to 1911. Brown was the ace of those dominant Cub teams, which won four pennants and two World Series in five years.

He was the Cubs' "money pitcher." Four of his five World Series wins were shutouts. His duels with Giant ace Christy Mathewson were electrifying. At one point, he owned Matty, beating him nine consecutive times.

The media, jumping on his handicap, called him "Three-Finger" Brown. His teammates called him "Miner," as he had worked in the coal mines before he became a big leaguer.

Brown was probably the best pitcher in the short history of the Federal League, going 31-19 in two years, and helping the Chicago Whales to the 1914 Federal League pennant.

LIFETIME STATS: W: 239, L: 130, Sv: 49, ERA: 2.06, SO: 1,375, CG: 271.

39. Ryne Dee "Ryno" Sandberg, 2B-3B-22, Phillies, Cubs, 1981–97.

Sandberg, a benchwarmer for the Phillies at the time, was a throw-in in the deal that sent Ivan DeJesus from the Cubs. It turned out to be a stunning deal for Chicago, who acquired the best second baseman of the 1980s.

Sandberg was a tremendous all-around player. He was a great fielder, winning a record nine consecutive Gold Gloves at second base. In 1986, he set a record for the fewest errors (five) and highest fielding percentage ever, with a .994 mark. In all, Sandberg had the best fielding percentage for a second baseman four times in his career. In 1989, he went 91 games without an error at second base, another record.

As good as he was in the field, Sandberg was also quite accomplished at the plate. He hit .300 or better five times in his career, and had 20 or more doubles 13 times, 19 or more home runs eight times, scored 100 or more runs seven times and racked up 100 RBI twice. In 1984, his MVP season, he was a triple and a home run short of being the first player ever to have 200 hits and 20 or more doubles, triples, home runs and stolen bases.

In 1990, Sandberg had another top shelf season, leading the league in home runs with 40, in runs scored with a league-leading 116, and hitting .306 with 30 doubles, 100 RBI and 25 stolen bases.

Sandberg was also one of the best-hitting Cubs in the postseason, hitting .385 in two League Championship series.

LIFETIME STATS: BA: .285, HR: 282, RBI: 1,061, H: 2,386, SB: 344.

40. Rodney Cline "Rod" Carew, 1B-2B-DH, Twins, Angels, 1967–85. Hall of Fame, 1991.

Carew was a hitting machine, turning in 15 consecutive .300 seasons in his 19-year career. Only Ty Cobb, Stan Musial and Honus Wagner ever exceeded that number.

In addition, Carew won seven batting titles, and won them by consistently larger margins than anyone in history except Rogers Hornsby. In 1977, the year he won the MVP Award, Carew hit .388. The next best average was Dave Parker's .338, which won the National League batting title. That 50-point margin is the greatest gap between the best and second-best hitters in major league history.

In 1972, he became the first player in history to win a batting crown without hitting a home run. Carew hit for the cycle in 1970 and, in five separate games over his career, got five base hits.

Besides hitting, Carew was one of the best base runners ever. He stole home seven times in 1969, and on May 18 of that year, stole three bases in one inning. In addition, he was probably one of the best players ever at taking the extra base on a single or a double.

Carew was not an outstanding defensive player, but he was solid. A misconception that has persisted after his retirement was that he was moved from second base to first base in 1976 because of his defensive liabilities. Actually, he was moved there to prolong his career. He was named to 18 consecutive All Star games, although he missed two with injuries.

LIFETIME STATS: BA: .328, HR: 92, RBI: 1,015, H: 3,053, SB: 353.

41. Brooks Calbert "Brooksie," "The Human Vacuum Cleaner" Robinson, 3B-2B-SS, Orioles, 1955–77. Hall of Fame, 1983.

Robinson was called "Brooksie" by his teammates and Oriole fans, but his unofficial nickname was "The Human Vacuum Cleaner" for his uncanny fielding abilities.

Robinson's play has set the standard to which all third basemen aspire. He won 16 consecutive Gold Gloves in his 23 years at third base. He led American League third basemen in fielding 11 times, including nine of 10 years from 1960–69 (the Tigers' immortal Don Wert beat him out in 1965). He led the league's third basemen in assists eight times and was a 15-time All Star.

Robinson didn't play baseball in high school, and was discovered by the Orioles playing in a church league. He sat on the bench for three years before becoming a regular in 1958. He was not an outstanding hitter, but he hit 20 or more home runs six times, batted .280 or better seven times and stroked 25 or more doubles 11 times in his career. In 1964, he hit .317, drove in a league-leading 118 runs and had 194 hits to win the MVP award.

His post-season performances have been legendary. Twice in League Championship Series in 1969 and 1970, he hit over .500. In the 1970 World Series, Robinson hit .429 and slugged .810 to win the MVP award (which included a late-model sedan) as Baltimore dominated a very good Cincinnati Reds team. "If we knew he wanted a car that badly," said Reds catcher Johnny Bench, "we'd have bought him one."

Robinson is the all-time leader at third base in games played with 2,870, fielding average with a .971 mark, putouts with 2,697, double plays with 618 and assists with 6,205.

LIFETIME STATS: BA: .267, HR: 268, RBI: 1,357, H: 2,848, SB: 28.

42. George Kenneth "The Kid" Griffey, Jr., OF-DH, Mariners, Reds, 1989–present

This may be a case of bad karma, or something. For a majority of his 11 years with the Seattle Mariners, "Junior" was by far the best player in the game. But in 2000, after signing with the Reds, three of the four years since have been injury-plagued.

Griffey broke in with Seattle as a baby-faced 19-year-old in 1989, and had a solid season, with 120 hits in 127 games, 23 doubles and 16 home runs. By the next year, he was a star, winning the first of 10 Gold Gloves in the outfield, hitting .300, with 22 home runs and 80 RBI.

He became the cornerstone of the Mariner franchise. Griffey has hit 40 or more home runs seven times, and in 1997 and 1998, had back-to-back seasons of 56 homers. In 1997, Griffey was the MVP, with the aforementioned 56 dingers, a .304 average, 34 doubles and a league-leading 125 runs scored, 147 RBI and 393 total bases.

Griffey has scored 100 or more runs six times, hit .300 or better seven times, and had 100 or more RBI eight times. Throughout the 1990s, Griffey was in the top 10 in MVP voting with Seattle.

In 2000, he was traded to the Reds, and had a decent season (for Griffey), with a .271 average, 40 homers, 118 RBI and 141 hits. But the injury bug smote Griffey as he passed his 30s, and he hasn't played close to a full season since.

LIFETIME STATS: BA: .294, HR: 481, RBI: 1,384, H: 2,080, SB: 177.

43. Willie Lee "Mac," "Big Mac," "Stretch" McCovey, 1B-OF-DH, Giants, Padres, Athletics, 1959–1980. Hall of Fame, 1986.

McCovey's major league debut with the San Francisco Giants in 1959 was an impressive one: 4-for-4 with two singles and two triples against future Hall-of-Famer Robin Roberts. McCovey didn't actually get into a game until the end of July, but despite playing only 52 games, he was still named Rookie of the Year, with a .354 average, and 13 home runs and nine triples in 52 games.

McCovey became a regular in the outfield, as the Giants already had a great first baseman in Orlando Cepeda. But in 1965, when Cepeda was felled by an injury, McCovey moved over to first and remained there for the rest of his time with the Giants.

McCovey, at 6'4", 210 pounds, was a tremendous physical specimen, and his home runs were usually explosive shots that got out of the park in a hurry. He won three home run crowns, in 1963 with 44, 1968 with 36 and 1969 with 45. The latter year, McCovey won the MVP award, with a league-leading 126 RBI, 26 doubles, 121 walks, 101 runs scored and a league-leading .656 slugging percentage.

McCovey is the only man to hit two homers in one inning twice in his career, in 1973 and again in 1977, but he is best known for a ball he hit that made an out. In the 1961 World Series, in the bottom of the ninth inning, with two outs, runners on second and third and trailing 1-0, McCovey hit a line drive that Yankee second baseman Bobby Richardson speared to end the game. It was, said McCovey, the hardest hit ball he had ever struck.

LIFETIME STATS: BA: .270, HR: 521, RBI: 1,555, H: 2,211, SB: 26.

44. Ronald Edward "Ron" Santo, 3B-DH, Cubs, White Sox, 1960–74.

Overshadowed by Brooks Robinson in the National League, Santo was nonetheless the best all-around third baseman in the National League throughout the 1960s. He won five consecutive Gold Gloves, from 1964 to 1968. Santo also led National League third basemen in putouts seven times, in double plays six times and in assists seven times. In 1964, he set a record (since broken) of assists by a third baseman with 367.

But Santo could also hit. He was not thought to be a power hitter, but Santo hit 25 or more home runs and drove in 90 or more runs in eight consecutive seasons, some of those years on Cubs teams that were notorious for their lack of hitting ability.

Santo led the league in bases on balls four times, but paradoxically, also struck out more than 100 times a season four times.

He was an intense guy, and was often very emotional after a big win or a tough loss. But Cub fans loved him for that and forgave some of his outbursts against umpires whom Santo thought might have given Chicago short shrift.

Oddly, Santo is best known for a quirky mannerism he displayed in 1969. As the Cubs began to make their ill-fated run toward a pennant, Santo would jump up and click his heels after every win.

Initially, it was simply a manifestation of his enthusiasm for finally being on a winning team. But of course, after a while, the fans demanded it, and other teams began to resent the move. It was all moot, of course, as Chicago fell short that year.

LIFETIME STATS: BA: .277, HR: 342, RBI: 1,331, H: 2,254, SB: 35.

45. Wade Anthony "Chicken Man" Boggs, 3B-DH, Red Sox, Yankees, Devil Rays, 1982–99.

Wade Boggs was a hitting machine for the Boston Red Sox in the 1980s and early 1990s. He had a beautiful, level swing, a superior eye for pitches in the strike zone and the patience to wait for the pitch he wanted to hit.

Boggs was mired for six years in the Red Sox minor league system, apparently because he was an indifferent fielder. But when he finally made it to Boston in 1982, Boggs was an immediate star, hitting a rookie record .349 with 118 hits in just 104 games.

In 1983, Boggs won his first batting title, hitting .361 with 210 hits, 100 runs scored, 44 doubles and 74 RBI. It was the first of seven consecutive years that he would go on to record 200 or more hits and 100 or more runs.

From 1983 to 1988, Boggs won the American League batting championship five of six years. In 1985, he led the league with 240 hits and a .368 batting average. He reached base 340 times that year, a feat only Babe Ruth, Ted Williams and Lou Gehrig have accomplished.

And his fielding improved, as well. In 1993 and 1995, while playing third base for the Yankees, he was the top fielding third baseman in the league. Boggs won back-to-back Gold Glove awards in 1994 and 1995.

Much was made of his metronome-like habits. His diet during the season was almost exclusively chicken, he took batting practice at 7:17 every night, and he walked to and from the dugout along exactly the same route. That intense concentration was clearly a key factor in Boggs' success.

LIFETIME STATS: BA: .328, HR: 118, RBI: 1,014, H: 3,010, SB: 24.

46. Gregory Alan "Greg" Maddux, RHP, Cubs, Braves, 1986–present.

Arguably the best pitcher of the 1990s and certainly the best hurler in the National League in that span. A 10-time Gold Glove winner for the Chicago Cubs and, later, the Atlanta Braves, Maddux was considered the best fielding pitcher in baseball in the 1990s. He won his first Cy Young award in 1992 with the Cubs, and then from 1993 to 1995, won three more for the Braves. Maddux is the only pitcher to win four consecutive Cy Young awards.

Maddux is called "The Thinking Man's Pitcher" because he changes speeds well, and has exceptional control. He led the Braves to the 1995 World Championship over Cleveland. Known as an "inning eater" because he often pitches into the eighth inning, thus eliminating the need for multiple relievers, Maddux has thrown 200 or more innings 15 times in his career.

Following the 2003 season, Maddux, now an aging veteran, signed with the Cubs to anchor a strong pitching rotation.

LIFETIME STATS: W: 289, L: 163, Sv: 0, ERA: 2.89, SO: 2,765, CG: 113.

47. James Alvin "Jim," "Jockstrap Jim," "Cakes" Palmer, RHP, Orioles, 1965–67, 1969–84. Hall of Fame, 1990.

Palmer played his entire career with the Orioles, and is Baltimore's greatest pitcher. But for the first four years of his career, he battled arm and back injuries that threatened to end that career.

Palmer was 23-15 in his first three years, but injuries forced him back to the minor leagues in 1968. Surgery and rehabilitation in the Instructional League helped him regain his form. Less than a week after he was called up in 1969, Palmer no-hit the Oakland A's.

For the next decade, except for an injury-filled 1974, Palmer was one of the most consistent hurlers in baseball. He won 20 or more games eight times. Only Walter Johnson had more 20-win seasons in the American League, with 12. Twelve times, Palmer struck out more than 100 batters and he pitched 300 or more innings four times.

Palmer won three Cy Young awards, in 1973, 1975 and 1976. He was also an excellent fielder, winning four Gold Gloves from 1976 to 1979.

Palmer was a legitimate big game pitcher. He participated in six American League Championship Series, and had a 4-1 mark with a 1.96 ERA. He also pitched in six World Series, and was 4-2 with 44 strikeouts in 64 innings.

LIFETIME STATS: W: 268, L: 152, Sv: 4, ERA: 2.86, SO: 2,212, CG: 211.

48. John Robert "Johnny," "The Big Cat" Mize, 1B-OF, Cardinals, Giants, Yankees, 1936–53. Hall of Fame, 1981.

Mize, called "The Big Cat" because he was, well, a pretty big cat, was a rarity in pro baseball: a slugger who was also a great contact hitter.

Twice in his career, Mize led the league in home runs, but had fewer strikeouts than dingers, a remarkable feat. In 1947, Mize led the league with 51 homers and struck out only 42 times in 586 at-bats. In 1948, Mize struck a league-leading 40 home runs and struck out only 37 times. In all, Mize would claim four home run crowns and a batting title in 1939, and lead the league in RBIs three times.

Mize is the only man to hit three home runs in a game six times. He also hit two home runs in 30 games. Mize had seven pinch-hit home runs in his career.

Mize was a four-time All Star for the Cardinals and a five-time All Star for the Giants, but in 1949, he was traded to the Yankees. From 1949 to 1953, Mize was a part-time first baseman and pinch hitter for the Bronx Bombers, and all five of those teams won pennants and subsequently won World Series.

He hit .286 in the five championship series, and was the World Series MVP in 1952, hitting three home runs and batting .400 as the Yankees beat the Dodgers.

Considered awkward, Mize was actually a graceful fielder, leading the league's first basemen in fielding twice, in 1942 and 1947.

LIFETIME STATS: BA: .312, HR: 359, RBI: 1,337, H: 2,011, SB: 28.

49. Michael Joseph "Mike" Piazza, C, Dodgers, Mets, 1992–present.

In 2004, Piazza became the all-time leader in home runs by a catcher. On May 5, 2004, he blasted his 352nd dinger, leaving him one ahead of Carleton Fisk. A superior athlete, Piazza has hit 30 or more home runs nine times in his career, and has hit 40 homers twice.

Piazza was drafted by the Dodgers, and brought up at the tail end of 1992. He played his first full season in 1993, and was named Rookie of the Year, on the basis of a .318 batting average, 35 home runs, 112 RBI, 24 doubles and 174 hits.

Piazza is a great all-around hitter. In addition to socking home runs, he has hit .300 or better nine consecutive seasons, from 1993 to 2001. A 10-time All Star, Piazza's .319 career batting average is fourth among active players and 55th all-time.

In 1996, he won the league MVP award, hitting .336 with 36 home runs, 105 RBI, 184 hits and 87 runs scored.

He was traded to the Mets in 1998, and, in 2000, was a key to New York's National League championship. Piazza batted .324 with 38 home runs, 113 RBI and 90 runs scored that season.

Piazza, when healthy, has been amazingly consistent. He generally hits between 35 and 40 homers a year, scores 80 to 100 runs, makes 150 to 200 hits and drives in 90 to 120 runs. He is generally a tough out in the post-season, and hit four home runs and five doubles in 10 games in the National League Championship Series win over the Cardinals and the World Series loss to the Yankees in 2000.

LIFETIME STATS: BA: .319, HR: 358, RBI: 1,107, H: 1,708, SB: 17.

50. Timothy "Tim," "Rock" Raines, OF-DH, Expos, White Sox, Yankees, Athletics, Orioles, Marlins, 1979–99, 2001–02.

When the lighting-fast Raines came up with the Montreal Expos, he was an explosive base-stealer who could change games without getting a hit. He led the league in stolen bases from 1981 to 1984 and was second in 1985 and third in 1986, averaging an eye-popping 76 thefts a year in that span.

The switch-hitting Raines was an excellent lead-off hitter, scoring 90 or more runs eight times and leading the league in that department twice. His 808 steals are fifth all-time. Raines won the batting championship in 1986. He hit .300 or better eight times in his career.

Raines was also a pretty patient man at the plate. He drew 80 or more walks seven times in his career. His 1,330 walks are 29th all-time.

Following a 12-year stint with the Expos, Raines was signed by the White Sox in 1991. By 1994, he was a part-time player for Chicago, but he was still a good hitter, if not as effective a base-stealer as he had been. Raines became a part-time player with the Yankees from 1996–1998 and seemingly finished up his career with the Oakland Athletics in 1999. But he made a comeback in 2001 with the Expos and did pretty well, hitting .308 in part-time play. He was traded to the Orioles that year and finally retired in 2002 after a year with the Florida Marlins.

LIFETIME STATS: BA: .294, HR: 170, RBI: 980, H: 2,605, SB: 808.

51. Mark David "Big Mac," "Sack" McGwire, 1B-3B, Athletics, Cardinals, 1986–2000.

McGwire became a home run hitting machine in the latter part of his career, hitting 135 dingers in a two-year span, from 1998 to 1999.

There is some speculation that the 6'5", 225-pound McGwire may have enhanced his already hefty frame with steroid use, but frankly, that's all it is: speculation.

Regardless of whether or not his performances were "juiced", McGwire was a most gracious home run champion. In 1998, when he was on track to best the 37-year-old record of 61 home runs by former great Roger Maris, McGwire invited the Maris family to be his guests (Maris died in 1985) for the several days it took to hit his 62nd, and when that moment finally came, McGwire dutifully acknowledged Maris. McGwire went on, of course, to hit 70 homers that year.

It's also easy to forget that McGwire won two home run crowns before his 70 homers in 1998 and 65 in 1999. He cracked 49 homers in his second year with the Athletics in 1987 and hit 52 with Oakland in 1996.

McGwire came up with the Athletics, and was always a big swinger. He had 100 or more strikeouts in eight seasons, including a whopping 155 the year he hit 70 home runs. But he also led the league in bases on balls twice, and had more than 100 walks four times in his career.

McGwire was relatively slow afoot, with only six career triples and 12 career stolen bases. But his supporters will argue that he was not paid to steal bases, McGwire was paid to hit the ball out of the park, which he did with regularity.

LIFETIME STATS: BA: .263, HR: 583, RBI: 1,414, H: 1,626, SB: 12.

52. Wilver Dornel "Willie" Stargell, OF-1B, Pirates, 1962–82. Hall of Fame, 1988.

Slugger Stargell was a fearsome opponent at the plate, looming over the batter's box, whipping his bat forward and back, forward and back, waiting almost eagerly for the next pitch.

Stargell was a big, powerful man at 6'2", 225 pounds. He belted some tape measure home runs, including seven that carried over the right field roof at Forbes Field, and the only two home runs ever hit out of Dodger Stadium.

A quiet, classy ballplayer, Stargell played, willingly, in the shadow of Pirate star Roberto Clemente for 10 years. But he became the Pirates' team leader after Clemente's sudden, stunning death in 1971. In 1979, Stargell won the MVP award in leading Pittsburgh to another World Series triumph over the Orioles.

Stargell's numbers that year were not overpowering: 32 home runs, 82 RBI, a .281 batting average. But he seemed to clock a majority of the key hits for Pittsburgh in the regular season. And in the World Series, Stargell killed Baltimore, with a .400 batting average, four doubles, three home runs and seven RBI. He was the leader of the Pirates' family, and the team song was "We Are Family" by Sister Sledge.

Thus, in addition to his MVP in the regular season, Stargell was the MVP of the National League Playoff Series against the Reds, the MVP of the World Series, The *Sporting News* Man of the Year and *Sports Illustrated's* co-sportsman of the year with the Steelers' Terry Bradshaw.

LIFETIME STATS: BA: .282, HR: 475, RBI: 1,540, H: 2,232, SB: 17.

53. Albert William "Al" Kaline, OF-DH, Tigers, 1953–74. Hall of Fame, 1980.

Kaline is also nicknamed "Mr. Tiger," in part because he holds the team record for games played with 2,834 and home runs with 399, and in part because he represented Detroit so well for his entire 22-season career.

Kaline was, initially, a small, shy kid who worked for virtually everything he earned on a baseball field. He was signed right out of a Baltimore sandlot league in 1953 and didn't play a game in the minors.

In 1954, Kaline's first full season in the majors, it was clear that he would be a solid defensive outfielder: he had a good arm and excellent instincts. But he built up his wrists and arms, reportedly from exercises suggested by Boston's Ted Williams, and by 1955, Kaline was a bona fide star. He won his only batting title that year, hitting .340, and stroked 200 hits, also tops in the league.

Kaline also smacked three home runs in one game at Kansas City that year, the only time in his career he would do so.

Kaline would hit .300 or better nine times in his career, and belt 20 or more home runs nine times.

He was one of the most graceful fielders of his era, and one of the best all time. Kaline earned 10 Gold Gloves in the outfield, and twice led the league in fielding percentage. In 1971, he played 133 games in the field without an error.

LIFETIME STATS: BA: .297, HR: 399, RBI: 1,583, H: 3,007, SB: 137.

54. Juan Antonio "The Dominican Dandy" Marichal, RHP, Giants, Red Sox, Dodgers, 1960–75. Hall of Fame, 1983.

Marichal was signed by the Giants in 1960, and was already a polished pitcher at age 19. Still, San Francisco brought the Dominican Republic native along slowly, as a sport starter. He went 6-2 with a solid 2.66 ERA.

In 1962, Marichal was a key performer in the Giants' National League championship team with an 18-11 mark, although he injured his foot and lost his last three decisions. But from 1962 to 1969, Marichal won 172 games and lost 76. That comes out to an average 21-9 record.

He led the league in wins, innings pitched, shutouts and complete games twice in that span, and in ERA once. The sturdy Marichal three times threw more than 300 innings in a season, leading the league in that category twice.

Marichal's high kick before his pitch was legendary, and also effective. It was distracting to hitters, and it made his fastball, slider and curve that much tougher to hit.

In August of 1965, in the heat of a tense pennant race with the Dodgers, Marichal got into a brawl with Dodger catcher John Roseboro, hitting Roseboro with his bat. A wild brawl ensued and when the smoke cleared, Roseboro was hospitalized with a concussion.

Roseboro subsequently sued Marichal for assault, but eventually dropped the suit.

Marichal retired in 1975, and after he was passed over for induction into the Hall of Fame, the classy Roseboro led a letter-writing campaign to install Marichal. It worked, and Marichal made it a point to thank Roseboro at his induction in 1983.

LIFETIME STATS: W: 243, L: 142, Sv: 2, ERA: 2.89, SO: 2,303, CG: 244.

55. Carlton Fisk, C, Red Sox, White Sox, 1969, 1971–93. Hall of Fame, 2000.

Fisk remains the best offensive catcher in baseball, with 1,276 runs scored, more than 100 more than any other back stopper, 3,999 total bases, far ahead of any other catcher, and more stolen bases (128) than Johnny Bench, Yogi Berra and Mike Piazza combined.

The first player to be voted Rookie of the Year unanimously, Fisk was a tremendous weapon for the Red Sox in the 1970s, hitting .290 or better five times and getting 100 or more hits six times. And how many catchers ever led the league in triples, as Fisk did in 1972, with nine? Fisk has more career triples (47) than Bench, Piazza and Roy Campanella combined. In 1972, he won a Gold Glove for his catching.

Fisk was injured for part of the 1975 season, but rebounded to hit .331 and lead Boston into the World Series against the Cincinnati Reds. He was the center of two of the key plays in the Series. The first came in the 10th inning of Game Three, when he collided with Ed Armbrister while trying to field a bunt. No interference was called on Armbrister, even though it was clear Fisk's ability to field the ball was impeded. The Sox lost that contest.

But in Game Six, he hit the most dramatic home run in Series history. He blasted a pitch by Red hurler Pat Darcy into the night in the 12th inning, and there probably aren't too many people who haven't seen Fisk jumping into the air, hands upraised, as the ball leaves Fenway Park.

He wasn't as effective with the White Sox, after he was traded there in 1981. But no matter where he was, Fisk was a clubhouse leader and a masterful handler of pitchers.

LIFETIME STATS: BA: .269, HR: 376, RBI: 1,330, H: 2,356, SB: 128.

56. Jeffrey Robert "Jeff" Bagwell, 1B, Astros, 1991–present.

Bagwell may be the best player no one realizes is a great player. The proof of this is that Bagwell has only been in four All Star games in the 1990s and was probably one of the top 15 players in that decade.

But check out some of his stats. Bagwell has hit 30 or more home runs nine times in his career. He's hit .300 or better six times, had 100 or more RBI eight times, scored 100 or more runs eight times and drawn 100 or more walks seven times. He's even pretty good on the base paths, having stolen 10 or more bases 10 times.

In fact, Bagwell, who won the MVP award in 1994, has finished in the top 10 of the MVP voting six times, which is more often than he has finished in the top voting for the All Star game. (Bagwell was second in MVP voting in 1999 and third in 1997.)

Bagwell is the fifth active player in terms of career total walks with 1,287, his home run total is the seventh-best among active players and his RBI total sixth best among active players. Not too many people outside of the Houston area code seem to know this.

LIFETIME STATS: BA: .300, HR: 419, RBI: 1,421, H: 2,137, SB: 196.

57. Saturnino Orestes Arrieta "Minnie," "The Cuban Comet" Minoso, OF, Cleveland, White Sox, Cardinals, Senators, 1949–1964, 1976, 1980.

In his first game with the White Sox in 1951, Minnie Minoso became the first black player to don a Chicago uniform in the history of the team. In the first inning of the game, he homered off Yankee pitcher Vic Raschi.

Minoso was a three-time Gold Glove winner who had consistently good numbers throughout his career. He led the league in stolen bases three times: in 1951, 1952 and 1953. In 1954, he led the league in triples, with 18, and a .535 slugging percentage. In 1957, Minoso led the league in doubles with 36. He also had no problems leaning into a pitch: he was hit by pitchers 192 times in his career, a league record.

Minoso is one of only two players (along with Nick Altrock) to have played in five decades. The record is something of a gimmick; he was activated for three games in 1976 (he went 1-8) and two more in 1980 (0-2).

LIFETIME STATS: BA: .298, HR: 186, RBI: 1,023, H: 1,963.

58. Barry Louis Larkin, SS, Cincinnati, 1986–present.

Larkin is one of the best all-around players in the 1990s, and, at 39, continues to play at a high level into the 21st century.

You want hitting? Between 1988 and 2000, 11-time All Star Larkin hit better than .300 nine times. Three other years, he hit .293 or better. You want baserunning? Larkin stole 40 bases in 1988 and 51 in 1995. His lifetime success ratio is 83 percent.

He is an excellent fielder, leading the league in 1994 with a .980 average, and only once dropping below .975. Larkin is a three-time Gold Glove winner. He was the league MVP in 1995, the year the Reds won the World Series. In 1996, he became the first shortstop ever to hit more than 30 home runs and steal 30 bases in the same season.

In the 1996 All Star game, Ozzie Smith, the best shortstop in the league, presented Larkin with an autographed bat and told him, "The torch is now officially passed."

LIFETIME STATS: BA: .295, HR: 190, RBI: 916, H: 2,240.

59. Frank "The Big Hurt" Thomas, 1B-DH, White Sox, 1990–present.

Here's a guy who, for the first eight years of his career, was just kicking ass and taking names. From 1990 to 1997, Thomas was a five-time All Star and the American League MVP in 1993 and 1994. And his numbers in the years before and after those two seasons weren't appreciably different.

In fact, in that 1990–97 span, he hit .300 or better every year; had 109 or more walks every year and was among the league leaders in on-base percentage and slugging percentage every season.

Since 1997, The Big Hurt's numbers have dipped: not alarmingly, but noticeably. He's still a pretty patient hitter who doesn't strike out much. But his path to the Hall of Fame, once a clear highway, was bumpier in 2003.

Thomas hit .353 in the American League Championship Series for the White Sox in 1993.

LIFETIME STATS: BA: .310, HR: 418, RBI: 1,390, H: 2,048.

60. Paul Leo "The Igniter," "Molly" Molitor, DH-3B-2B-1B-SS-OF, Brewers, Blue Jays, Twins, 1978–98. Hall of Fame, 2004.

Molitor was one of the most versatile players in the majors during his first decade as a player. For the first three years of his career with the Brewers, Molitor was the team's starting second baseman, and also played shortstop and third base. He was switched to third base in 1982, and played there, for the most part, over the next seven years, but also played shortstop, second base and the outfield.

Molitor was moved to the designated hitter slot more or less permanently in 1991, but was also used at first base for as many as 40 games a season. This was less because of any defensive liability, and more to protect Molitor from injury.

At the plate, he was Mr. Consistency. He hit .300 or better 12 times, scored 90 or more runs eight times, topped 190 hits six times and five times scored 100 runs or more. A total of 13 times in his career, Molitor stole 20 or more bases. In 1987, Molitor had a 39-game hitting streak.

Molitor is 10th lifetime in doubles with 605, ninth lifetime in hits with 3,319, 11th lifetime in sacrifice flies with 109 and 17th lifetime in runs scored with 1,782.

Molitor has been outstanding in the post-season. He has hit .368 in five series, including .418 in two World Series. In 1993, in the Blue Jays' win over the Phillies, Molitor was 12 for 24 with two home runs, two doubles and 10 runs scored to win the MVP award.

LIFETIME STATS: BA: .306, HR: 234, RBI: 1,307, H: 3,319, SB: 504.

61. Lynn Nolan "The Ryan Express" Ryan, RHP, Mets, Angels, Astros, Rangers, 1966–93. Hall of Fame, 1999.

The strikeout king, with 5,714. Nobody else is even close. A model of consistency and durability, Nolan Ryan pitched for 27 years in the big leagues, finally retiring at age 46.

Somehow, people have the impression that Ryan's numbers are misleading. Until late in his career, when he punched out a league-leading 301 batters at age 42 in 1989, the "book" on Ryan was that he wasn't a winner. (He was a World Series winner: The 1969 Mets.) Certainly many of his teams weren't successful, but Ryan, an eight-time All Star, won 324 games in his career. He struck out 300 or more batters in six separate seasons and has thrown a major league record seven no-hitters. He broke Sandy Koufax's single season record of 382 strikeouts, getting 383 in 1973.

LIFETIME STATS: W: 324, L: 292, Sv; 3, ERA: 3.19, SO: 5,714, CG: 222.

62. Robin Evan Roberts, RHP, Phillies, Orioles, Astros, Cubs, 1948–66. Hall of Fame, 1976.

Robin Roberts in 10 words or less: "Hated to come out; let 'em hit the ball."

The seven-time All Star remains the winningest righthander in the history of the Philaelphia Phillies. He won 20 games or more six years in a row, from 1950 to 1955 and from 1952 to 1955 led the league in wins. He also led the league in complete games from 1952 to 1956 and pitched 300 or more innings for six seasons in a row, from 1950 to 1955.

A lanky righty with a smooth motion, Roberts also gave up a lot of home run balls, although it often seemed that most of them occurred with the bases empty. Still, he gave up a major league record 46 dingers in 1956. Roberts wasn't quite as dominant after the early to mid-1950s, and struggled with arm trouble for a while. But he bounced back in 1962 to 1964, winning 37 games for Baltimore.

LIFETIME STATS: W: 286, L: 245, Sv; 25, ERA: 3.41, SO: 2,357.

63. Gary Edmund "The Kid" Carter, C, Expos, Mets, Giants, Dodgers, 1974–92. Hall of Fame, 2003.

The ebullient Carter was one of the most popular players in the 1970s and 1980s, and one of the best catchers in that span, as well.

The 11-time All Star was the anchor of the Montreal Expos in the 1970s and early 1980s. Between 1977 and 1982, Carter led National League catchers in most chances six times, putouts six times, assists five times and double plays four times.

He was traded to the Mets in 1984, and led New York to the 1986 World Championship. His single in the 10th inning of Game Six of that World Series was one of the key blows in that amazing three-run rally.

Carter won three Gold Gloves during his career, but many believe his fielding was vastly underrated, probably because he was such a good hitter. Carter was also well known for being a good handler of younger pitchers.

LIFETIME STATS: BA: .262, HR: 324, RBI: 1,225, H: 2,092.

64. Billy Leo Williams, OF-DH-1B, Cubs, Athletics, 1959–76. Hall of Fame, 1987.

Billy Williams was the quiet assassin for the Chicago Cubs for 17 years. Often overshadowed by teammate Ernie Banks, Williams was nonetheless one of the most durable players in National League history, playing in a record 1,117 consecutive games, a National League mark later broken by Steve Garvey in 1983.

Williams had a lovely swing that Hall-of-Famer Rogers Hornsby recognized immediately. At Williams' first tryout with the Cubs, Hornsby deemed the soft-spoken Williams as major league material immediately.

The six-time All Star won a batting crown in 1972, at age 34. He hit 20 or more home runs 13 years in a row and 14 out of 15 seasons.

LIFETIME STATS: BA: .290, HR: 426, RBI: 1,475, H: 2,711.

65. Richard Anthony "Dick" Allen, 1B-3B, Phillies, Dodgers, Cardinals, White Sox, Athletics, 1963–77.

Dick Allen was one of the greatest athletes in the history of the game. He was also, hands down, one of its greatest enigmas.

Immensely talented, often incredibly contradictory, Allen generated as much newsprint for his eccentric behavior as for his ballplaying abilities.

He was a seven-time All Star. He hit better than .300 seven times, socked 20 or more home runs 10 times, and was the American League MVP in 1972. But in 1974, he was on his way to another big year when he "retired" for no good reason—or at least for no reason he would tell anyone about.

Allen feuded with coaches and with fans. Interestingly, he got along, for the most part, with his teammates, who knew enough to let him alone. It adds up to a very good career, but one that probably could have been much better.

LIFETIME STATS: BA: .292, HR: 351, RBI: 1,119, H: 1,848.

66. Ferguson Arthur "Fergie" Jenkins, RHP, Phillies, Cubs, Rangers, Red Sox, 1965–83. Hall of Fame, 1991.

As a pitcher, Jenkins was durable, athletic and consistent. Yet during his playing years, he rarely got the credit he deserved.

Jenkins won 20 games or more six years in a row and seven years out of eight between 1967 and 1974. From 1967 to 1972, he won 127 games for the

Cubs. In that span, Chicago had seven 20-game winners: Jenkins (six times) and Bill Hands. In other words, it was Ferguson Jenkins and a cast of dozens. Five times, he pitched more than 300 innings in a season.

Yet Jenkins was named to only three All Star teams. He won the Cy Young Award in 1971, but he won more games in 1974, struck out more men in 1969 and 1970 and held opponents to lower batting averages in 1968, 1969 and 1970.

Jenkins won 284 games in his career and struck out 3,192.

In 1991, Jenkins became the first Canadian born player to be inducted into the Hall of Fame.

LIFETIME STATS: W: 284, L: 226, Sv: 7, ERA: 3.34, SO: 3,192.

67. Roberto "Robby," "Bobby" Alomar, 2B-DH, Padres, Blue Jays, Orioles, Indians, Mets, White Sox, 1988-present.

Bobby Alomar is a 12-time All Star with 10 Gold Glove awards on his resume. In addition he is an excellent hitter, with nine seasons hitting .300 or better.

He's been a member of two World Champ teams, in Toronto in 1992 and 1993. Orlando Cepeda once compared Alomar favorably to Joe Morgan, Rod Carew and Cool Papa Bell.

Truthfully, he doesn't hit as well as Morgan or Carew, but he's close. And he doesn't run as well as Bell, but maybe nobody ever did. Suffice to say that Alomar has played at a high level from the 1990s into this century.

His biggest problem is that when people think of Robby Alomar, they don't think of Gold Gloves or .300 seasons. They remember the last weekend of the 1996 season when a frustrated Alomar spat on umpire John Hirschbeck. It's sort of the curse of ESPN, if you will. But Alomar is a good one who could be a great one if he keeps it up.

Alomar hit .400 or better in three postseason series: the 1991 ALCS, the 1992 ALCS and the 1993 World Series.

LIFETIME STATS: BA: .301, HR: 206, RBI: 1,110, H: 2,679.

68. Donald Arthur "Don" "Donnie Baseball" Mattingly, 1B, Yankees, 1982–95.

Unlike many superstars who play a year or two (or three) beyond their time, Mattingly is the one guy who should not have retired when he did.

Donnie Baseball was playing pretty well at the end of the 1995 season, but he felt he could not perform up to the standards that he had set, and left baseball. The next season, the Yankees won their first World Championship in 18 years. There is not a Yankee fan alive who doesn't wish the classy Mattingly had hung around.

He was great. He won nine Gold Gloves, a record for first basemen. He was a six-time All Star. He was MVP of the league in 1985 and probably should have won it again in 1986 (Boston's Roger Clemens beat him out).

But by 1992, his back was bothering him and it began to get tough to play. Still, he hung in there for three more years, and always played hard. In his only post-season series, a loss to the Seattle Mariners, Mattingly acquitted himself well, hitting .417 with six RBI.

LIFETIME STATS: BA: .307, HR: 222, RBI: 1,099, H: 2,153.

69. Osborne Earl "Ozzie," "The Wizard of Oz" Smith, SS, Padres, Cardinals, 1978–96. Hall of Fame, 2001.

It's almost impossible, on a statistical basis, to judge which individual might have been the greatest defensive player at his position. Fielding averages don't measure range, or arm accuracy. But it's very hard to dismiss Smith as at least the best defensive shortstop ever.

He was a 15-time All Star and a 13-time Gold Glove winner. Smith was not an overpowering hitter. But he made 100 hits or more 17 consecutive years and stole 580 bases for his career. His post-season numbers are good, but not great, except for 1982, when he hit .556 in the National League Championship Series against the Braves.

LIFETIME STATS: BA: .262, HR: 28, RBI: 793, H: 2,460.

70. Luis Ernesto "Little Louie" Aparicio, SS, White Sox, Orioles, Red Sox, 1956–73. Hall of Fame, 1984.

Luis Aparicio began playing professionally when he was just a teen, in his native Venezuela. His personal coach was perhaps the greatest shortstop in the history of the Venezuelan Leagues, Luis Aparicio, Sr.

Luis Jr. was signed by the White Sox, who were so confident he would make it, they traded the incumbent, Chico Carrasquel. Chicago's confidence was not misplaced. Aparicio became a nine-time Gold Glove winner at shortstop and led the American League in stolen bases for nine consecutive seasons, from 1956-64.

He teamed with second baseman Nellie Fox to give the White Sox a tremendous double-play combination. They led Chicago to the team's first pennant since the 1919 "Black Sox."

Aparicio was a steady but not overpowering hitter. He hit over .300 only once, in 1970. But he had 20 or more doubles 14 times in his career.

LIFETIME STATS: BA: .262, HR: 83, RBI: 791, H: 2,677.

71. Dale Bryan Murphy, OF-1B, Braves, Phillies, Rockies, 1976–93.

Murphy was one of the best players in the game in the 1980s, becoming the youngest player ever to win back-to-back MVP awards in 1982 and 1983.

Murphy started his major league career as a catcher, but was eventually moved to the outfield with the Braves. He was low-key, likeable and a great hitter. A seven-time All Star, he twice led the league in home runs, in 1984 and 1985.

Murphy was primarily a slugger, but he was patient, leading the league in walks in 1985 and three other times topping 90 bases on balls.

He was a five-time Gold Glove winner in the out-field. He also could run a little, and in 1983 stole 30 bases and hit 36 home runs, placing him in the elite "30-30" category.

Murphy played in 740 consecutive games from September of 1981 to July of 1986.

LIFETIME STATS: BA: .265, HR: 398, RBI: 1,266, H: 2,111.

Top 10 Position Players (1900–1950)

1. George Herman "Babe" Ruth, P-OF-1B, Red Sox, Yankees, Braves, 1914–35. Hall of Fame, 1936

It's time to face facts: Fifty-five years after his death, 69 years after his retirement, 80 years after he first played in the big leagues, there is still no one like Babe Ruth.

A couple of years ago, various publications and media outlets published those "50 Greatest Athletes" lists, and Ruth was always the top baseball player. Whether he was better than Jim Thorpe or Muhammed Ali on the all-time athlete list is still debatable. Whether he's the best baseball player isn't.

He started off not as a pitcher, but as a left-handed catcher for the St. Mary's Industrial School for Boys. He was a big kid, fresh off the streets of Baltimore. He found structure and baseball at St. Mary's. He also found another position, as some unknown St. Mary's coach eventually moved him onto the mound.

He signed with the Baltimore Orioles, by now a pitcher, and on one of his first days in spring training, one of the veteran Orioles asked another just who that tall, left-handed drink of water was. That, said the other player, was Baltimore manager Jack Dunn's "baby." And so he was.

Dunn shipped him to Boston, where, by 1915, his second year in the league, Babe Ruth was the best left-handed pitcher in the American League and probably in baseball. Ruth's duels with the Washington Senators' Walter Johnson were classics of the 1910s.

Had Ruth spent his entire career on the mound, he would doubtless have set a number of pitching records. But 1915 was also the year he hit his first home run, a towering shot against New York pitcher Jack Warhop on May 5. He found that he enjoyed it.

Ruth, of course, eventually switched to the outfield, so he could play every day. And he rewrote the record books. Not only did he hit 60 home runs in 1927, but Ruth was the first player to hit 30 homers, the first to hit 40 and the first to hit 50, as well.

He was stylish, he was colorful. In 1930, Ruth signed for $80,000 per year, a figure that brought his annual salary to $5,000 more than President Herbert Hoover. A reporter asked Ruth how he could justify making more than the president of the United States of America.

"Well," said Ruth, "I had a better year than he did."

He is now in the lexicon of American speech, as well. Feats of great importance or athleticism are now "Ruthian." That is perhaps the greatest tribute of all.

LIFETIME STATS: BA: .342, HR: 714, RBI: 2,213, H: 2,873, SB: 123. W: 95, L: 46, Sv: 4, ERA: 2.28, SO: 488, CG: 107.

2. Johannes Peter "Honus" Wagner, SS-OF-1B-3B, Louisville, Pirates, 1897–1917. Hall of Fame, 1936.

The story goes that one day in Pittsburgh, Wagner was manning his shortstop position when he reached around with his glove hand to pull out a chaw of tobacco from his back pocket. (In the early days of baseball, players wore gloves that more closely resembled golf gloves.) The batter hit a sharp grounder his way. Wagner calmly bare-handed the ball and gunned it over to first, thus throwing out a man with one hand behind his back.

Wagner was stocky, barrel-chested and had shovels for hands. Legend has it that when he dug balls out of the infield dirt and zipped them over to first base, a small load of stones and dirt would travel with the ball.

He played virtually every position except catcher. He was a tremendous hitter, winning eight batting titles and six slugging average titles. He hit over .300 16 times, led the league in doubles seven times and triples three times. He stole 722 bases, and led the league in that category five times.

In 1902, Wagner played 61 games in the outfield, 44 at shortstop, 32 games at first base, one at second base and pitched once. He didn't make an error at any of those positions. From 1913 to 1916, he led the league's shortstops in fielding position.

Wagner was a terrific athlete: He may well have been the first baseball player to lift weights, and he was a fanatic about a new game that had recently been invented in Springfield called basketball. He played baseball until he was 43 and was perhaps the best 40-year-old player in baseball history.

LIFETIME STATS: BA: .327, HR: 101, RBI: 1,732, H: 3,415, SB: 722.

3. Tyrus Raymond "Ty" Cobb, OF-1B, Tigers, A's, 1905–28. Hall of Fame, 1936.

Seventy-five years after he retired from baseball, Ty Cobb still owns the best career batting average of all time: .366. And he still holds the distinction of being the nastiest SOB of all time. There are no stats for that; Cobb has retired the trait.

Be that as it may, the man could hit: a total of 12 batting championships, including five in a row from 1911 to 1915. He had back-to-back .400 seasons in 1911 and 1912, with another .400 season in 1922, and more than 4,100 career hits, a record that stood for 50 years.

Cobb wasn't a slugger in the present sense of the word, but he still had a career slugging percentage of .512, and led the league in that category eight times.

And he could run: 892 stolen bases, leading the league six times. He was the all-time leader until Lou Brock passed him in 1978.

Was he mean? Yeah, he was mean. He used to sharpen his spikes in the dugout as opposing teams took batting practice, and he wasn't afraid to jab a slow-footed infielder when sliding into second or third base. He had more than his share of fights, and in 1912, went into the stands after a heckling fan.

He's known to have cheated. According to pitcher Dutch Leonard, he paid off Cleveland's Tris Speaker and Joe Wood to throw a game to the Tigers so Detroit could finish third. He may have tried to fix other games, but it was impossible to determine.

Cobb, were he alive today, would probably say that he played to win, at any cost. He did. And it paid off. In 1936, he was the top vote-getter for the first class of the Baseball Hall of Fame, topping Babe Ruth, Cy Young and Honus Wagner.

LIFETIME STATS: BA: .366, HR: 117, RBI: 1,937, H: 4,189, SB: 892.

4. Joshua "Josh" Gibson, C, Homestead Grays, Pittsburgh Crawfords (Negro Leagues), 1929–46. Hall of Fame, 1972.

He was a stellar player in a legendary league. He was Josh Gibson, "the Black Babe Ruth," the greatest catcher of all time, the best position player in Negro League history.

His numbers are stratospheric. He is credited with 962 home runs over his long career, although there were several years in which he played a Negro League season and then headed south to play in either the Dominican League or the Mexican League. Still, 962 home runs are 962 home runs. Author John Holway's statistical analysis of the Negro Leagues credits Gibson with 224 in Negro League play.

He is credited with 84 homers in 170 games in 1936, which includes non-Negro League contests. He hit 75 homers in 1931 and 69 in 1934. He is credited with hitting a ball nearly out of Yankee Stadium when the Grays played an exhibition game there one year.

His .351 batting average in Negro League play is the third-highest of all time. Gibson would routinely hit .400 or better in winter league play. In 1937, Gibson hit .479 in the Puerto Rican League. He was elected to nine Negro League All Star teams, where he hit an amazing .483 in All-Star contests.

Defensively, Gibson was extremely quick, with a rifle arm. He was also a good base runner, and exceptionally fast for a catcher.

Gibson was a big man, at 6'1", 210 pounds. His easy-going nature was often interpreted as ignorance or low intelligence by writers and even fellow Negro League players. But it's hard to believe a dumb guy could be such a great player.

In 1943, Gibson suffered a nervous breakdown, and his skills eroded quickly after that. He had begun to drink and probably also took drugs. He was still a good player for the next few years, but he was no longer the greatest. Early in 1947, he suffered a fatal stroke.

LIFETIME STATS: BA: .351, HR: 224, H: 1,010.

5. Tristam E. "Tris," The Grey Eagle," "Spoke" Speaker, OF-1B, Red Sox, Indians, Senators, A's, 1907–28. Hall of Fame, 1937.

Tris Speaker was the best two-way player of his generation. He was not as great a hitter as Ty Cobb, but was a better defensive player by miles and miles and a better teammate by a greater margin than that.

Speaker lived a legendary life. He broke his right arm as a youngster, so he learned to hit and throw left-handed. He started out as a pitcher. Scouts were interested, but his mother refused to sign his contract (Speaker was only 17), believing that buying and selling players was an insult. She eventually came around.

After he signed his first professional contract, Speaker hopped a freight car to the minor league town he signed with to save money. Speaker arrived literally an hour before the game and was told by his manager he was the starting pitcher. He lost the game, 2–1.

He was eventually converted into an outfielder but the Red Sox thought so little of him, they didn't send him a contract the year after he signed. He reported anyway. The Sox still didn't want him, and left him behind in spring training, as payment to the Little Rock minor league team for the use of their ball field. He stuck around and dominated the Southern League. The Sox finally decided they liked him, and brought him up in 1907.

He was a great hitter, winning the batting crown in 1916, and hitting .345 lifetime.

But he was an unearthly fielder. Blessed with great speed, he played the shallowest center field anyone could remember. Several times in his career, he completed unassisted double plays—that is, he would catch a line drive and run over second base to double up the runner. Amazing. He remains, 66 years after his retirement, the all-time baseball leader in double plays by an outfielder (139), as well as assists (449).

And he was a winner, with two world championships in Boston and the first ever title in Cleveland in 1920.

LIFETIME STATS: BA: .345, HR: 117, RBI: 1,529, H: 3,514, SB: 432.

6. Louis Henry "The Iron Horse" Gehrig, 1B, Yankees, 1923–39. Hall of Fame, 1939.

Lou Gehrig was the best first baseman, ever. A couple players come close, including Jimmie Foxx and, in the modern era, Mark McGwire. But neither can really match Gehrig's tremendous production, year after year after year.

The story of how Gehrig began his amazing longevity streak of 2,130 consecutive games has, in the 21st century, undergone several permutations.

He did replace Wally Pipp on May 31, 1925, and Pipp did indeed have a headache. But manager Miller Huggins didn't exactly hand the position to Gehrig after Pipp sat out. Huggins pinch-hit for Lou several times in June and in fact, Gehrig did not start at first base for New York on July 5 of that year (Pipp did), but got in for a couple of innings late in the game.

But Lou was hitting well and Pipp wasn't, so Huggins left him in the rest of the year. And, of course, the year after that and the year after that, and, you get the idea.

Gehrig hit for average and he hit for power. He won three home run crowns, in 1931, 1934, and 1936. In that 1934 season, he won the Triple Crown with a .363 batting average, 49 homers and 165 RBI. He was MVP in 1927 and 1936.

Huggins used to say he thought Gehrig was actually a more dangerous hitter than Babe Ruth because he could use more of the field than Ruth. Gehrig also tended to hit line drives, which scared the hell out of his opponents.

In 1939, his health began to fail. Rumors abounded, and he finally traveled west to the Mayo Clinic. The diagnosis was almost too cruel to believe: amyotrophic lateral sclerosis, to be known forever after as Lou Gehrig's disease.

Gehrig was fading so fast, that Lou Gehrig Day was held on July 4, 1939. It is the most famous ceremony in baseball history, with Gehrig declaring, "Today, I consider myself the luckiest man on the face of the earth." Maybe he was. He died two years later.

LIFETIME STATS: BA: .340, HR: 493, RBI: 1,995, H: 2,721, SB: 102.

The greatest right-handed hitter in baseball history was also one of its biggest curmudgeons.

Hornsby was a joy to watch. He stood at the back of the batter's box and executed a perfectly level swing that delivered the baseball to all corners of the field. In the early part of his career, Hornsby had some speed; he was quick out of the batters' box, and would always take the extra base against an unwary outfielder.

Hornsby led the league in doubles four times, in triples twice, in home runs twice, and in RBI four times. His Triple Crown year in 1922 was one of the greatest seasons any player has ever had in baseball history: His .401 batting average, 42 homers, 152 RBI, 46 doubles, 250 hits, 141 runs scored. .459 on-base percentage and .722 slugging average were all league leaders. And his .967 fielding percentage was the best in either league for a second baseman. He also had a 33-game hitting streak that year.

His .424 batting average in 1924 was the highest average in baseball history after 1900 (four players before that year did post better averages). Only Ty Cobb's lifetime batting average tops Hornsby's .358.

But Hornsby could be, well, difficult. He was very confident of his ability and had no problem reminding teammates or his manager of it. Hornsby had a major issue when dealing with authority, and often quarreled with managers and front-office types. As good as he was, that was not a good idea, and he was traded four times in his career.

He also had a whopper of a gambling problem. It didn't seem to affect him much in his early career, but it got worse as he got older. He managed the Cubs from 1925 to 1926, and was known to hit up his players for loans to cover his gambling losses. Again, not a good idea.

He ended his career with the St. Louis Browns, and, as he got older, he coached for several organizations, and seemed to mellow a bit. Still, Chicago Cub great Billy Williams will always remember his first tryout with the Cubs. The Rajah was overseeing it, and, when the tryout was over, Hornsby pointed to Williams and budding third baseman Ron Santo. Those two, Hornsby, said, will play in the big leagues. The rest of you, Hornsby said, might as well go home. And of course, Williams conceded, Hornsby was right. Except for Santo and him, none of the other players made it.

LIFETIME STATS: BA: .358, HR: 301, RBI: 1,584, H: 2,930, SB: 135.

Charleston had a barrel chest and spindly legs, and played the outfield, which drew comparisons to white slugger Babe Ruth. But he was closer to Ty Cobb as a hitter and to Tris Speaker as a defensive player. What it all meant was that

Charleston is believed by some to be the greatest all-around player in Negro League history.

Charleston was born in Indianapolis in 1896. After a stint in the Army, Charleston joined the Indianapolis ABCs as a pitcher-outfielder. Eventually, he was moved to the outfield permanently, and he soon became a star.

Charleston was an exceptional hitter with good power. Available records show him putting together back-to-back .400 seasons in 1924 and 1925, while playing for the Harrisburg Giants of the Eastern Colored League.

He was also an aggressive base runner. Several times, playing for several leagues over the years, Charleston would lead the circuit in stolen bases and home runs. Tales of Charleston's baserunning never fail to emphasize that he was not afraid to slide into opponents with his spikes high, much like his white contemporary, Ty Cobb.

Defensively, Charleston's exceptional speed enabled him, like Speaker, to play a very shallow center field. He, like Speaker, would often snag a line drive and run over to second base to double up the runner.

In 1931, Charleston was the best player on one of the best, if not the best, Negro League teams of all time, the Homestead Grays. Charleston played center field and hit .351. In a nine-game "world championship" series against another all-time great team, the Kansas City Monarchs, the Grays won the series, five games to four, and Charleston hit .511.

As he grew older and his legs began to bother him, Charleston moved from center field to first base. But he could still hit. Playing for another all-time great team, the 1935 Pittsburgh Crawfords, Charleston hit .294 and led the team to another Negro League World Series win over the New York Cuban Stars.

Charleston was coveted by white big league managers and owners, and no wonder: He holds the all-time record with 18 home runs in games between Negro League teams and white major league teams. But he came along a little too early to break into the major leagues.

LIFETIME STATS BA: .330, HR: 169.

9. James Emory "Jimmie," "Double X," "The Beast" Foxx, 1B-3B-C, A's, Red Sox, Cubs, Phillies, 1925–45. Hall of Fame, 1951.

The prototypical slugger of the 1920s and 1930s, Jimmie Foxx was called "the right-handed Babe Ruth" when he toiled for the A's.

Foxx didn't actually get his career started until 1929, four years after he was signed by the A's. That's because Connie Mack's A's were so deep that Foxx, who started out as a catcher, was sitting behind future Hall-of-Famer Mickey Cochrane for several years. When Mack finally moved Foxx to first base, he displaced veteran Jimmy Dykes.

But it was worth it. In Foxx's first full season as a starter, he led the American League in on-base percentage, and batted .354 with 33 home runs and 118 RBI. To top it off, the A's displaced the mighty New York Yankees as American League champions, and won the 1929 World Series over the Cubs. Foxx hit .350 in that Fall Classic, and added a pair of home runs.

In 1932, Foxx smacked 58 home runs, two short of Ruth's record. A's' fans like to point out that Foxx hit two home runs in games that were eventually rained out. Foxx won back-to-back MVP awards in 1932 and 1933. The latter season, he won the Triple Crown, with 48 home runs, 163 RBI and a .356 batting average.

In 1938, after he was traded to the Red Sox, Foxx had another sensational season, leading the league with a .349 batting average, 175 RBI, 119 walks, a .462 on-base percentage and a .704 slugging percentage. His 50 home runs were second in the league to Hank Greenberg's 58. But Foxx won the MVP.

He was a big dude. At six feet and 195 pounds, Foxx had huge upper arms and a powerful chest. Foxx would cut back the sleeves on his uniform so pitchers could see those biceps. He also had a great throwing arm and in fact pitched in 10 games in the majors, including two starts with the Phillies in 1945. His career record is 1-0 with a 1.52 ERA.

Foxx was also a very good teammate. He was especially kind to rookies, and Red Sox great Ted Williams recalled fondly how Foxx encouraged him and helped him when he was starting out in Boston.

LIFETIME STATS: **BA: .325, HR: 534, RBI: 1,922, H: 2,646, SB: 87.**

10. Melvin Thomas "Master Melvin," "Mel" Ott, OF-3B-2B, Giants, 1926–47. Hall of Fame, 1951.

Mel Ott was a coach's nightmare at the plate. He had a "foot in the bucket" batting stance, in which he raised his right leg just as he swung the bat, and then hooked upward as he completed his swing.

But Ott was a heck of a lot more effective than a lot of guys who had better-looking swings. He was the first National League player to hit 500 home runs, and held the record until fellow Giant Willie Mays broke it in 1967. Ott led the league in homers six times in his career.

He also had an excellent eye in the batter's box, leading the league six times in walks, and holding that record, as well, until Joe Morgan broke it in 1982.

Ott was signed by the Giants as a 15-year-old and by the time he was 16, he was sitting on the Giants' bench. New York coach John McGraw loved Ott's athleticism, and initially wasn't quite sure where to play the kid. So he had Ott working out at third base, second base and in the outfield. Eventually, the outfield was where Ott would see a majority of action throughout his career.

Ott was a wet-behind-the-ears 19-year-old when he became a regular in the Giants' outfield. The New York papers joshingly called him "Master Melvin" in reference to his age and schoolboyish looks.

There was nothing boyish about the way Ott played, however. He hit .322, with 26 doubles and 18 home runs in his first full season. The next year, he socked 42 home runs and had 151 RBI, both career highs.

McGraw didn't really like the leg kick, but he never tried to change Ott, because it was clear that the leg kick gave Ott that much more power. At 5'9", and between 170 and 180 pounds during his career, Master Melvin needed a little help.

Born in Louisiana, Ott was the classic Southerner. He was a gentleman in a game where gentlemen were the exception rather than the rule. In fact, Ott was the player to whom famed Dodger coach Leo Durocher referred when he uttered his famous quote, "Nice guys finish last." It was untrue in Ott's case: He played in three World Series, and hit .389 with two home runs as the Giants won the 1933 world championship.

LIFETIME STATS: **BA: .304, HR: 511, RBI: 1,860, H: 2,876, SB: 89.**

72. Alan Stuart Trammell, SS-DH, Tigers, 1977–96.

One of the great all-around players of the 1980s. The six-time All Star hit .300 or better seven times and won four Gold Gloves while holding down the shortstop position for Detroit for most of his 20 seasons in a Tiger uniform.

Trammell was a self-made superstar. He was not a good hitter initially, but his tireless work ethic in the off-season paid off. His anemic home run totals in the first six years of his career steadily improved until he popped a career-high 28 in 1987.

He was a good base runner. His 30 steals in 1983 were the most by a Tiger shortstop since a fellow named Cobb stole 34 in 1917.

Trammell was MVP of the 1984 World Series with a .450 average and nine hits in five games.

LIFETIME STATS: BA: .285, HR: 185, RBI: 1,003, H: 2,365.

73. David Mark "Dave" Winfield, OF-DH, Padres, Yankees, Angels, Blue Jays, Twins, Indians, 1973–95. Hall of Fame, 2001.

At 6'2" 220 pounds, big Dave Winfield looked like an All Star. Which he was, having been named to the All Star team 12 times.

Winfield didn't put up explosive numbers most of his career, but he was, when healthy, incredibly consistent. He never won a home run crown, but socked 465 in his career. He never had more than 193 hits in a season, but ended up with 3,110.

Winfield was also a stellar fielder, winning seven Gold Glove awards. His outfield arm was one of the most accurate in the game, although ironically, that arm gained most of its notoriety when Winfield accidentally killed a seagull with a throw in Toronto.

However well he played, though, team success eluded Winfield until he was traded to Toronto in 1992. In his one year with the Blue Jays, Winfield played in the outfield and was a DH for the World Champions.

LIFETIME STATS: BA: .283, HR: 465, RBI: 1,833, H: 3,110.

74. Thurman Lee "Tugboat," "Squatty Body," "The Wall" Munson, C-OF, Yankees, 1969–79.

Munson, despite what Reggie Jackson may claim, was the anchor of those late 1970s Yankee teams that won three AL titles in a row.

Munson was squat and looked a little dumpy in uniform, but that hid an athlete's body. He was one of the fastest catchers of all time and was very quick. He was one of the best in the league at covering bunts.

Munson, a seven-time All Star, hit over .300 in five seasons, and won three Gold Glove awards. He was league MVP in 1976, when he hit .302 with 105 RBI and 17 home runs as the Yankees won their first pennant of the 1970s.

Munson was still a fine ballplayer in 1979, but on August, 2 of that year, the plane he was piloting crashed near Cleveland, killing him. Munson hit .373 in World Series play.

LIFETIME STATS: BA: .292, HR: 113, RBI: 701, H: 1,558.

75. Andre Nolan "The Hawk" Dawson, OF-DH, Expos, Cubs, Red Sox, Marlins, 1976–96.

Dawson was a solid performer while with the Expos: a three-time All Star who hit .300 or better three times during his tenure with Montreal, possessing excellent power.

He was also an excellent fielder, winning six consecutive Gold Gloves with the Expos, from 1980 to 1985. The Hawk could run, too, stealing 20 or more bases seven times while in Montreal.

But Dawson was traded to the Cubs in 1987 and took things up a notch. That first year, Dawson smacked a league-leading 49 home runs and added a league-best 137 RBI. Dawson also hit .287 with 24 doubles.

The numbers won him the MVP award, even though there were some grumblings that Dawson was playing with a last-place team. He remains the only MVP winner to play for a cellar-dweller.

Dawson was named to the All Star team five times in Chicago, and hit .300 or better twice more. He also won two more Gold Gloves, in 1987 and 1988. In 1993, it was on to the Red Sox, where he had two more good years, primarily as a designated hitter.

LIFETIME STATS: BA: .279, HR: 438, RBI: 1,591, H: 2,774, SB: 314.

76. Keith "Mex" Hernandez, 1B-OF, Cardinals, Mets, Indians, 1974–90.

Hernandez won 11 consecutive Gold Gloves at first base, from 1978 to 82 with the Cardinals and from 1983 to 88 with the Mets. He was one of the best-fielding first basemen of all time.

His strength in the field was his amazing range. The agile six-footer led the league's first basemen in assists five times, putouts four times and fielding percentage twice. He is second to Eddie Murray in assists all-time with 1,682.

But Hernandez could also hit pretty well. In his 17-year career, Hernandez hit .290 or better 11 seasons. In 1979, he won the batting title, hitting .344 with St. Louis. That same year, his on-base percentage was .417, second-best in the league, and his 116 runs scored topped the circuit. Those stats, plus his stellar fielding, earned him the MVP award that year.

Hernandez was a key contributor to the Mets' championship drive in 1986, hitting .310 during the regular season and leading the league in walks. In fact, his on-base percentage was above .400 six times in his career.

LIFETIME STATS: BA: .296, HR: 162, RBI: 1,071, H: 2,182, SB: 98.

77. William Nuschler "Will the Thrill" Clark, 1B-DH, Giants, Rangers, Orioles, Cardinals, 1986–2000.

The rangy Clark hit .300 or better four times for the San Francisco Giants. He hit a career-high 35 home runs for San Francisco in 1987, and drove in a career-high 116 runs in 1991.

In the late 1980s, Clark was one of the best players in the National League. He finished in the top five in the MVP voting three years in a row, from 1987 to 1989. He led the league in RBI in 1988 with 109 and led the league in runs scored in 1989 with 104.

In the 1989 National League Championship Series against the Cubs, Clark was phenomenal, hitting .650 in five game, with 13 hits, eight RBI, three doubles, a triple and two home runs.

In 1991, Clark hit .301 with 116 RBI, 29 home runs and 32 doubles. He also won his only Gold Glove at first base.

A trade to Texas saw Clark continue his solid hitting. Clark spent five years with the Rangers and hit .300 or better four times, although his power numbers dropped.

LIFETIME STATS: BA: .303, HR: 284, RBI: 1,205, H: 2,176, SB: 67.

78. Kirby Puckett, OF-DH, Twins, 1984–1995. Hall of Fame, 2001.

Puckett was built like a fireplug with legs, and generated tremendous power from that relatively small frame. As a 23-year-old rookie with the Twins in 1984, Puckett hit .296 with 165 hits in 128 games.

He became the ninth player in major league history to debut with four hits in a nine-inning game, and his 16 assists from the outfield led the league.

Puckett had a little trouble figuring out big league pitching, and didn't hit a home run in his first season, and only socked four in 1985. But he clearly figured things out by 1986, and belted 31. After that, Puckett hit 12 or more home runs eight of the next nine years.

In 1989, he won his only batting title, hitting .339. But Puckett hit .300 or better eight times in his career, and in fact hit .325 or better five times. Five times, he made 200 or more hits, leading the league four times.

Puckett didn't look particularly graceful when he ran, but he still managed to collect six Gold Glove awards. He was also a better base-stealer than he gets credit for, swiping 10 or more bases seven times.

LIFETIME STATS: BA: .318, HR: 207, RBI: 1,085, H: 2,304, SB: 134.

79. James Edward "Jim" Rice, OF-DH, Red Sox, 1974–89.

Rice, in the late 1970s, was a one-man wrecking ball for the Red Sox. He came up in 1975, along with fellow rookie Fred Lynn. That season, Lynn got all the headlines, winning the Rookie of the Year and the MVP award. But while Lynn had a hard time duplicating his first season, Rice, who was no slouch himself in 1975, just seemed to get better and better.

In 1978, he was MVP, and deservedly so. Although this was also the year that the Yankees' Ron Guidry was 25-3, Rice was, day in and day out, the best player in either league. He hit .315, with a league-leading 46 home runs, 139 RBI, 15 triples and 213 hits. His 406 total bases were the highest in the league since Joe DiMaggio's 418 in 1937.

Rice hit .300 or better seven times in his career, had 20 or more homers 11 times, 100 or more RBI eight times and 200 or more hits four times.

He hit .333 in his only World Series in 1986 (he broke his wrist just before the 1975 playoffs), with six runs scored.

Rice was relatively slow afoot, and had a penchant for grounding into double plays. He grounded into 36 doubles in 1984, a major league record at the time.

LIFETIME STATS: BA: .298, HR: 382, RBI: 1,451, H: 2,452, SB: 58.

80. Donald Scott "Don" Drysdale, RHP, Dodgers, 1956–69. Hall of Fame, 1984.

The towering (6'6") Drysdale was an intimidating presence on the mound, for several reasons. First, he was a sidearm pitcher with excellent control. His delivery meant the ball came at batters from a difficult angle. Second, Drysdale was not afraid, and in fact was happy, to pitch inside on batters.

Drysdale set a 20th century record by hitting 154 batters, and led the league in that department a record five times. He would often refer to his knockdown pitches as "kisses".

But Drysdale was much more than a knockdown artist. He led the league in strikeouts three times, and had 200 or more strikeouts in a season six times. A workhorse who hated to come out of games, he pitched 300 or more innings in a season four times.

He also led the league in shutouts in 1959. In 1968, he threw six consecutive shutouts, and a since-broken 58 2/3 shutout innings.

An excellent hitter, Drysdale twice tied the major league record for home runs by a pitcher, with seven. His career total of 29 is second all-time. In 1965, he hit .300 and was one of the best pinch-hitters on the Dodgers.

Drysdale was a terrific pitcher in the All Star game, with a 2-1 mark overall, and a record 1.40 ERA with 19 strikeouts.

LIFETIME STATS: W: 209, L: 166, Sv: 6, ERA: 2.95, SO: 2,486, CG: 167.

81. Lawrence Eugene "Larry" Doby, OF, Indians, Tigers, White Sox, 1947–59. Hall of Fame, 1998.

Doby is now an historical asterisk, which is unfortunate. The first black player to play in the American League (Jackie Robinson integrated baseball in the National League), Doby was also a very good player: an excellent hitter and a sure-handed outfielder with great range.

He was signed by the Cleveland Indians in 1947, just four months after the Dodgers signed Robinson. Doby was surely subjected to as many racial indignities as Robinson, but his low-key demeanor did not attract as much media attention.

Prior to his signing, Doby was a budding star in the Negro Leagues, hitting .341 and .414 in his first two years with the Newark Eagles.

Doby, like Robinson, preferred to let his playing talk for him. He hit .301 to lead the Indians to the World Championship in 1948 and picked up the pace in the World Series, hitting .318.

Doby led the AL in home runs (32) and RBIs (126) in 1954, and finished a close second to Yogi Berra in the MVP voting. In Cleveland's pennant-winning year of 1954, Doby again led the league in homers with 32 and in RBI with 126. Five times in his career, Doby had 100 or more RBI.

Doby's big swing left him vulnerable to strike-outs, and in fact, he fanned 100 or more times four times in his career.

LIFETIME STATS: BA: .283, HR: 253, RBI: 970, H: 1,515, SB: 47. (MLB stats only)

82. Alexander Emmanuel "A-Rod" Rodriguez, SS-3B, Mariners, Rangers, Yankees, 1994–present.

Rodriguez began his professional career as an 18-year-old rookie with the Seattle Mariners. By 1996, when he was 20, he won the batting title with a .358 average, and also led the league in doubles with 54 and runs scored with 141. Oh, and he also belted 36 home runs and had a 123 RBI. Since then, he has only gotten better.

Rodriguez led the American League in home runs three consecutive seasons, from 2001-03. He has led the league in runs scored three times, total bases three times, in hits once and RBI once. He has slugged over .600 five times in 10 seasons. This is not your average shortstop.

In 2003, he won his first MVP award with the Rangers, hitting .298, with 47 home runs, 118 RBI, 30 doubles and 364 total bases. He also won his second consecutive Gold Glove award.

But Rodriguez has been frustrated by a lack of postseason play. As of 2003, he has never played in a World Series. But in a blockbuster trade just prior to the 2004 season, he was sent to the defending American League champion Yankees. Rodriguez was shifted to third base, in deference to Yankee captain Derek Jeter, who plays shortstop. But this is the best chance he has had for a championship.

LIFETIME STATS: BA: .308, HR: 345, RBI: 990, H: 1,535, SB: 177.

83. Jacob Nelson "Nellie," "Little Nel" Fox, 2B-3B, Athletics, White Sox, Astros, 1947–65. Hall of Fame, 1997.

Fox was a part-time player for three years with the Athletics, and had a relatively unremarkable career there. But he was traded to the White Sox, and his career took off. Fox became Chicago's regular second baseman, and was hard to dislodge, playing in 798 consecutive games there from Aug. 7, 1956 to Sept. 3, 1960.

But more than his durability, Fox was a tremendous defensive second baseman. Six times, he led second basemen in fielding percentage, and he won three Gold Gloves. He teamed up with Chico Carrasquel and later Luis Aparacio to give Chicago a strong defensive presence in their middle infield.

Fox had six seasons where he hit .300 or better, and he also led the league in hits four times. Six times, he made 190 or more base hits.

Not necessarily a threat to steal bases, Fox was nonetheless aggressive on the base paths. He stroked 20 or more doubles 11 times and 10 or more triples four times. He led the league in triples with 10 in 1960.

Fox was very tough to strike out. He never had more than 18 strikeouts in a full season, and ended up with only 216 on his career.

LIFETIME STATS: BA: .288, HR: 35, RBI: 790, H: 2,663, SB: 76.

84. Philip Henry "Phil" Niekro, RHP, Braves, Yankees, Indians, Blue Jays, 1964–87. Hall of Fame, 1997.

When the 48-year-old Niekro finally retired, he was the oldest player to perform regularly in the major leagues. Niekro rode his mastery of the quirky knuckleball into the Hall of Fame.

The 300-game winner was consistent and durable throughout his 24-year career. He won 20 games only three times, and led the league in that department only once, in 1974 when he was 20-13.

Because the knuckler didn't take a lot out of his arm, Niekro was durable. He threw over 300 innings four times, and tossed more than 250 seven other times. He led the league in complete games four times, with a career-high of 23 in 1979.

Niekro also has a lot of success striking out batters with the knuckler. He led the league with 262 punchouts in 1977, and had 190 or more strikeouts four other times.

Yet his prowess, perhaps because it was with the knuckler, was often taken for granted. He was chosen for only five All Star games, and only pitched in two, throwing a total of 1^{1}/3 innings.

Yet he pitched well, for good teams and not-so-good teams. At age 43, he was 17-4 for the Braves and led the league with an .810 winning percentage. In 1984 and 1985, he was a solid 32-20 for the Yankees.

LIFETIME STATS: W: 318, L: 274, Sv: 29, ERA: 3.35, SO: 3,342, CG: 245.

85. Fredric Michael "Fred" Lynn, OF-DH, Red Sox, Angels, Orioles, Tigers, Padres, 1974–90.

Wow. How about that first season, huh?

Fred Lynn burst into the limelight in Boston with a stunning season in which he won the Rookie of the Year award and MVP, a feat never accomplished before or since.

And he deserved it. Lynn hit .331, slugged a league-leading .556, with 47 doubles and 103 runs scored, also league bests. He also had 21 homers and 105 RBI.

Lynn's swing was tailor-made for the left-field wall in Fenway Park, but he was no slouch on the road, either. On June 18 of his rookie season, he drilled three homers and had 10 RBI and 16 total bases against the Tigers.

In his six years in a Boston uniform, Lynn hit .300 or better four times (and hit .298 in 1978), won a batting title in 1979 with a .333 mark, hit 124 home runs and made the All Star team every year.

His failure to keep up that standard was actually a tribute to his hustle. Lynn was also an amazing defensive outfielder, but his all-out play often had him slamming into walls. He was frequently injured his last few years with the Sox, and when he was finally signed by the Angels, he wasn't the Fred Lynn of old.

He was certainly pretty decent, however. Lynn hit .299 with 21 home runs for the Angels in 1982, and .287 in 1986 with the Orioles. He made the All Star team three times with California.

LIFETIME STATS: BA: .283, HR: 306, RBI: 1,111, H: 1,960, SB: 72.

86. Louis Rodman "Lou," "Sweet Lou" Whitaker, 2B-DH, Tigers, 1977-95.

In the field, Whitaker made defensive plays that were seemingly effortless, leading critics to decide he wasn't trying. Well, he had to be doing something right: he ranks ninth all-time among second basemen in runs scored (1,386) and RBI (1,084).

Whitaker was the Rookie of the Year in 1978, hitting .285 with 58 RBI and 71 runs scored. A down year in 1980, in which he hit only .233 with one home run, led many Tiger fans to conclude that he was something of a fluke. But Whitaker erased all that criticism over the next decade, making the All Star team five consecutive times and in 1983, hitting .320 and becoming the first Tiger to make 200 or more hits since 1943.

His power numbers steadily increased, and in 1985, Whitaker set a team record for second basemen with 21 home runs. He later shattered that mark with 28 in 1989. In all, Whitaker hit 20 or more home runs four times for the Tigers.

Defensively, Whitaker led the league's second basemen in fielding average twice, in 1982 and again in 1991. He was usually among the leaders in most defensive categories throughout the 1980s.

In the World Series of 1984, which the Tigers won over the Padres, Whitaker led the team with six runs scored and two doubles.

As the 1990s dawned, Whitaker was used as a part-time player more and more. But he was still effective, hitting .290, .301 and .293 in his last three seasons.

LIFETIME STATS: BA: .276, HR: 244, RBI: 1,084, H: 2,369, SB: 143.

87. Darrell Wayne Evans, 3B-1B-DH, Braves, Giants, Tigers, 1969–89.

The power-hitting Evans was one of the best third basemen of his era, and was the first player to hit 40 home runs in both leagues.

Evans came up with Atlanta in 1969, becoming the Braves' regular third baseman by the 1971 season. That was the season he first wore contact lenses, and Evans credits that adjustment with helping him improve.

By 1973, he was an All Star, hitting .281 with 41 homers, 104 RBI and a league-leading 124 walks. He and teammates Henry Aaron (40), and Davey Johnson (43), became the first teammates to hit 40 or more home runs in the same season.

Evans usually batted third, ahead of Aaron, and was on first base on April 8, 1974, the day Aaron belted home run Number 715 to break Babe Ruth's record. A patient hitter, Evans led the league in walks twice and five times had 100 or more.

He was traded to Detroit in 1984, and led the league in home runs with 40 the following year, his only home run crown. But he was one of the cornerstones of the Tigers' World Championship team of 1984.

LIFETIME STATS:
BA: .248, HR: 414, RBI: 1,354, H: 2,223, SB: 98.

88. Craig Alan Biggio, 2B-C-OF-DH, Astros, 1988–present.

Biggio is one of the most durable, smartest and most talented players in the league. He plays primarily second base, but for his first three years in Houston, he was primarily a catcher. In 1991, he was named to the All Star team, as he hit .295, scored 79 runs and had 23 doubles.

But the next season, Biggio was converted to second base, and hit 32 doubles, scored 96 runs and batted .277. He again made the All Star team, and would be an All Star a total of seven times.

Biggio has hit .290 or better seven times, stolen 20 or more bases nine times and hit 20 or more doubles 14 times, leading the league in 1994 (44 doubles), 1998 (51) and 1999 (56). Biggio does not have a lot of power, but he has socked 15 or more home runs nine times.

Biggio is tough to double up, having hit into an average of nine double plays a year. In 1997, he played all 162 games without hitting into a double play.

Biggio is also a tough cookie. He has been hit by a pitch 10 or more times a total of 10 years in his career. In 1997, the same year he didn't ground into a double play, he was hit a total of 34 times without missing a game.

LIFETIME STATS: BA: .287, HR: 210, RBI: 931, H: 2,461, SB: 389.

89. Atanasio "Tony," "Doggie" Perez, 1B-3B-DH, Reds, Expos, Red Sox, Phillies, 1964–86. Hall of Fame, 2000.

Perez was an RBI machine for most of his career. He only hit .300 or better three times in a 23-year career, but drove in 90 or more runs 12 times.

Perez was a first baseman for his initial three years with the Reds, from 1964 to 1966. He was moved over to third base from 1967 to 1971, to make room for Lee May. But he was moved back to first in 1972, where he remained for most of the rest of his career.

Perez was one of the cornerstones of the "Big Red Machine" of the 1970s. His job was to drive in runs, and nobody did it better in that span. He hit 20 or more home runs nine times, and his RBI totals from 1967 to 1976 never fell below 90.

Perez was a pretty good fielder, as well, leading National League first baseman in fielding percentage in 1974 with a .996 mark.

In the post-season, Perez usually shone, even if his numbers weren't always outstanding. He hit only .179 against the Red Sox in 1975, for example, but three of his five hits in the series were home runs, including a solo blast in Game Seven. He had 10 hits in the 1972 series loss to Oakland.

Following the 1976 season, Perez wandered around the big leagues, spending three years each in Montreal and Boston, and a year in Philadelphia before returning to Cincinnati to retire.

LIFETIME STATS: BA: .279, HR: 379, RBI: 1,652, H: 2,732, SB: 49.

90. Graig "Puff" Nettles, 3B-OF, Twins, Indians, Yankees, Padres, Braves, Expos, 1967–88.

Nettles was an acrobatic, power-hitting third baseman who showcased his talent with the New York Yankees from the mid-1970s to the mid-1980s.

Nettles started out as an outfielder for the Twins at the beginning of his career, but by the time he got to Cleveland, he was manning third. Nettles proved how wise that move was by leading the league's third basemen in fielding percentage. In 1971, he set an American League record with 412 assists and 54 double plays.

He was traded to the Yankees at the start of the 1973 season, and had problems adapting. His average fell to .234 and he fielded poorly. But he rebounded over the next few seasons, and was named to the All Star team in 1975.

Nettles was one of the leaders of the Yankees' three consecutive American League champions from 1976 to 1978. He led the league in home runs with 32 in 1976, and won Gold Gloves in 1977 and 1978.

His defensive play in 1977 was amazing. In Game Three of the World Series, Nettles made three diving stops of line drives that preserved a 5–1 Yankee win over the Dodgers. Los Angeles coach Tommy Lasorda said later that Nettles' defensive play that night was the greatest individual effort he had ever seen.

Nettles' production dropped off in the early 1980s, and he was traded to the Padres. But there, at age 40, he and ex-teammate Goose Gossage helped San Diego to the National League pennant.

LIFETIME STATS: BA: .248, HR: 390, RBI: 1,314, H: 2,225, SB: 32.

91. Gaylord Jackson Perry, RHP, Giants, Indians, Rangers, Padres, Yankees, Braves, Mariners, Royals, 1962–83. Hall of Fame, 1991.

The (alleged) master of the spitball, and various other illegal pitches, Perry was the first player to win the Cy Young award in both leagues.

Perry was signed by the Giants, and spent four unremarkable seasons there as a spot starter. In 1966, Perry got off to an amazing start, at one point owning a 20-2 record, before tailing off to a very solid 21-8 mark. Still, he earned a berth in the All Star game, the first of five.

Perry won 20 or more games twice with the Giants, but slumped to 16-12 in 1971, and was traded to the Indians. But in 1972, Perry led the league with 24 wins, five shutouts and 342 $2/3$ innings pitched. It was good enough to win his first Cy Young award. After a stint with the Texas Rangers, Perry was traded again, this time to the San Diego Padres.

Perry had a masterful first season with San Diego, going 21-6, with a 2.73 ERA, 154 strikeouts and 260 $2/3$ innings pitched. He easily won his second Cy Young that year.

Perry had an assortment of pitches, including a good curve and a live slider. But over the years, allegations surfaced that he also doctored the ball, using spit, or Vaseline, or grease or something.

Perry was constantly moving on the mound, touching his cap, his uniform, his hair, and was often searched by umpires, who never found anything. All those shenanigans were, more often than not, used by Perry to distract the batter.

LIFETIME STATS: W: 314, L: 265, Sv: 11, ERA: 3.11, SO: 3,534, CG: 303.

92. Maurice Morning "Maury" Wills, SS-3B, Dodgers, Pirates, Expos, 1959–72.

Wills was actually a pretty decent hitter who was also a pretty good infielder, but he is most remembered for his phenomenal success in stealing bases in the early 1960s.

Wills came to the Dodgers in 1959, and shared the shortstop duties with veteran Don Zimmer. Wills was pretty unspectacular, but Zimmer wasn't a heck of a lot better, so Wills became the regular second baseman for Los Angeles in 1960.

He took off, hitting .295 and leading the league in stolen bases with 50. In 1961, Wills scored 105 runs and stole 35 bases, again leading the league.

By now, Wills was a bona fide weapon for the Dodgers. In 1962, he stole a stunning 104 bases, hit .299, had 208 hits, scored 130 runs and had a league-leading 10 triples to edge Willie Mays and win the MVP award.

Wills' 104 stolen bases shattered Ty Cobb's old record of 96. More importantly, Wills was caught stealing only 13 times in 1962, Cobb was caught 38 times in 1915.

Wills led the league in stolen bases three more years after 1962, and stole 25 or more bases five more times, including 52 for the Pirates in 1968.

Wills, by the way, was a pretty good defensive shortstop. He won two Gold Gloves, in 1961 and again in 1962.

LIFETIME STATS: BA: .281, HR: 20, RBI: 458, H: 2,134, SB: 586.

93. Willie Larry Randolph, 2B, Pirates, Yankees, Dodgers, Athletics, Brewers, Mets, 1975–92.

Randolph played a handful of games with the Pirates before being traded to the Yankees in 1976, which was technically his rookie year. He was so highly regarded that year that he was on the All Star ballot as a rookie and eventually made the team.

Randolph was the quiet member of the tumultuous New York Yankees teams of the late 1970s. He didn't feud with owner George Steinbrenner, he didn't snipe at teammates in the papers, he didn't pout when he was in a slump. He just played. And he played very well.

The Yankees won three consecutive pennants from 1976 to 1978 with Randolph at second base, including two World Championships. Randolph was a very consistent player for New York, hitting around .275, scoring 70 runs and stealing 30 bases in that span.

In the 1980s, when the Yankees began to flounder, Randolph continued to play well. He hit .294 in 1980, and led the league with 119 walks.

From 1982 to 1987, Randolph never hit below .276, averaged 20 doubles, 82 runs scored and 80 walks a season, and played well in the field. He made six All Star teams in his career.

After the 1988 season, Randolph was signed by the Dodgers. He was mostly a part-time player there, and finished up his career with three teams in his last two years, including 90 games with the Mets in 1992.

LIFETIME STATS: BA: .276, HR: 54, RBI: 687, H: 2,210, SB: 271.

94. Ivan "Pudge" Rodriguez, C-DH, Rangers, Marlins, Tigers, 1991–present.

Rodriguez is the best defensive catcher in baseball right now, and one of the best of all time.

Rodriguez has won 10 Gold Gloves for his fielding as a catcher. In 1999, he was the MVP of the American League, hitting .332, with 35 home runs, 113 RBI, 116 runs scored and 25 stolen bases.

Rodriguez was a 10-time All Star in Texas, from 1992 to 2001. He hit better than .300 eight times, socked 10 or more home runs 10 times and had 20 or more doubles nine times.

When he was signed by the Florida Marlins, it was considered a major coup for the fledgling franchise, which had had exactly one winning season since 1993. That was, admittedly, a big one, as it was 1997, the year the Marlins won the World Championship.

In 2003, Rodriguez helped make the Marlins two-for-two in winning seasons and World Championships. He hit .297, with 16 home runs, 36 doubles, 85 RBI and 90 runs scored.

The Marlins defeated the Giants in the Divisional Championship Series, and Rodriguez hit .353. In the League Championship Series against the Cubs, Rodriguez hit .321 with two doubles, two homers and 10 RBI. He won the series MVP award as he rallied the Marlins from a 1-3 hole to win the National League pennant.

In the World Series, Rodriguez hit .273, but cracked two doubles as the Marlins stunned the New York Yankees.

Prior to the 2004 season, Rodriguez was traded to the Tigers. Rallying this team toward .500 will be an uphill task, but one Rodriguez seems ready for.

LIFETIME STATS: BA: .304, HR: 231, RBI: 914, H: 1,875, SB: 90.

95. Pedro Jaime Martinez, RHP, Dodgers, Expos, Red Sox, 1992–present.

From 1997 to 2000, Martinez was, without a doubt, the best pitcher in baseball. That may not necessarily be true in 2004, but Martinez is at least in the top three, which isn't too shabby.

In the aforementioned four-year span, Martinez has won three Cy Young awards, in 1997 with Montreal and in 1999 and 2000 with Boston. He has led the league three of those four years in lowest ERA, including two years when it was under 2.00.

Martinez, at 5'11", 175, is not a big man, but up until 2003, he had a blistering fastball that had tremendous movement. In 1997, his first Cy Young year, Martinez became the first right-handed pitcher since Walter Johnson in 1912 to strike out more than 300 batters and have an ERA under .200.

In 1999, his second Cy Young year, he had eight 10-strikeout games and beat every American League opponent at least once. In 1999, Martinez became the first pitcher since Nolan Ryan to strike out 10 or more batters in seven consecutive starts.

In 2000, Martinez set a modern major league record for allowing opponents the lowest batting average over a season (.167).

Those numbers are impressive, but since that span, Martinez has struggled with injuries, although he was second in the Cy Young voting in 2001 and third in 2002. But he is reinventing himself on the mound. He now longer blows teams away with velocity, and has been putting more movement on the ball. Entering his 30s, Martinez is showing that he is a canny veteran who can still get the job done much more often than not.

LIFETIME STATS: W: 166, L: 67, Sv: 3, ERA: 2.58, SO: 2,426, CG: 41.

96. David Gene "Dave," "The Cobra" Parker, OF-DH, Pirates, Reds, Athletics, Brewers, Angels, Blue Jays, 1973–91.

The imposing (6'5", 230 pounds) Parker was a part-time player for his first two seasons in Pittsburgh, but he moved into the starting lineup in 1975. That year, he belted 25 home runs, 35 doubles and 10 triples to go with 101 RBI.

Dubbed "The Cobra" because of his intimidating bat speed, Parker won back-to-back batting titles in 1977 and 1978, with averages of .338 and .334, respectively. He never won a home run crown, but twice led the league in doubles with 44 in 1977 and 42 in 1985.

He won the MVP award in 1978, with 30 homers, 117 RBI and 194 hits to go with the batting title.

Despite being a very large man, Parker was a pretty good base stealer, swiping 20 bases twice and 10 or more five other times.

During his tenure with the Pirates, Parker was also an excellent defensive outfielder. He had a cannon arm from right field, and won three Gold Glove awards from 1977 to 1979.

But his size and weight caused leg and knee injuries, and Parker's effectiveness began to wane. He was traded to the Reds in 1984, and had two good years out of four there, and then bounced around with five teams in four years before retiring.

LIFETIME STATS: BA: .290, HR: 339, RBI: 1,493, H: 2,712, SB: 154.

97. Anthony Nomar Garciaparra, SS, Red Sox, 1996–present.

Nomar, or as they call him in Beantown, "Nom-ah," is the best hitting shortstop in the majors, with a lifetime career average of .323.

Garciaparra started slowly in Boston, hitting only .241 in limited duty in 1996, but on September 1, in his first major league game, he gave a hint of things to come, going 3-for-5. He also hit four homers in 24 games.

In Garciaparra's first full season in 1997, he hit .306, and led the AL with 209 hits and 11 triples. His 684 at bats is a Red Sox season record. He also became the first player to hit double figures in doubles (44), triples (11) and home runs (30), since Jim Rice did it in 1978.

Garciaparra won back-to-back batting titles in 1999 (.357) and 2000 (.372). He flirted with the .400 mark, and was still hitting .403 as late as July 20 and .398 as late as July 28.

He has battled injuries to his wrist and legs, but has still managed to be a consistent performer at the plate. He has had 190 or more hits six times in his career. Garciaparra has had a 24-game hitting streak in 1998 and a 21-game streak in 2000.

In the post-season, he has hit .400 in two separate series.

LIFETIME STATS: BA: .323, HR: 173, RBI: 669, H: 1,231, SB: 82.

98. Derek Sanderson Jeter, SS, Yankees, 1995–present.

Jeter is one of the premiere shortstops in baseball and one of the best post-season players ever.

Jeter has hit .300 in six of his nine seasons, and hit .291 in 1997 and .297 in 2002. But he is the quintessential Yankee; statistics mean very little to Jeter. His principal focus is on wins and losses.

In that category, he has few peers. Jeter has played eight full seasons. His Yankee teams have been in the post-season every year. He has played in six World Series, winning four. Jeter has never lost a League Championship Series, going 6-0.

Certainly, the Yankees are far from a one-man team. But Jeter is the sparkplug. In the overall post-season, Jeter is hitting .314. In seven of the 20 post-season series in which he has participated, Jeter has hit .400 or better. Jeter has 123 hits in 99 games in the post-season. He was the MVP of the League Championship Series and the World Series in 2000.

Jeter has scored 100 or more runs seven times, hit 20 or more doubles eight times and stolen 20 or more bases five times.

LIFETIME STATS: BA: .317, HR: 127, RBI: 615, H: 1,546, SB: 178.

99. Joseph Paul "Joe" Torre, C-1B-3B, Braves, Cardinals, Mets, 1960–77.

Torre was one of the most versatile players of the 1960s. He started out as a catcher with the Braves, and finished second behind Billy Williams in the Rookie of the Year voting. In 1963, he became Milwaukee's regular catcher, and hit .293 with 14 homers and 71 RBI.

The next season, his stats improved, even though he split his time between catching and playing first base. Torre hit .321, with 20 homers and 109 RBI, led all catchers in fielding percentage and again made the All Star team. Torre won a Gold Glove in 1965, and hit 27 home runs. In 1968, he led the league's catchers in fielding with a .996 mark.

Torre was traded to St. Louis, and, after a year, became the Cardinals' starting third baseman. He responded with a tremendous season in 1971; leading the league with a .363 batting average, 137 RBI and 230 hits, Torre easily won the MVP Award. He also led the league's third basemen in putouts.

After two years at third, the Cardinals moved Torre back to first base, and he hit .280 or better for the next three years. He was traded to the Mets in 1975, and hit .306 while splitting time between first and third base.

LIFETIME STATS: BA: .297, HR: 252, RBI: 1,185, H: 2,342, SB: 23.

100. Donald Howard "Don" Sutton, RHP, Dodgers, Astros, Brewers, Athletics, Angels, 1966–88. Hall of Fame, 1998.

Sutton was a smart, tough pitcher who knew his limitations and parlayed that knowledge into a Hall-of-Fame career.

Sutton began his career with the Dodgers, and was named Rookie of the Year in 1966, when his 209 strikeouts were the most by a first-year player since Grover Cleveland Alexander's 227 in 1911. Sutton struck out 200 or more batters five times in his career.

Sutton played in the shadow of other Dodger greats, such as Sandy Koufax and Don Drysdale, for several years. But by 1971, with a 17-12 record, 194 strikeouts and four shutouts, Sutton was the ace of the staff.

Sutton was always in tremendous condition, and it served him well. He played 23 years in the bigs, and never spent a day on the disabled list, and his durability enabled him to become the first pitcher ever to win 300 or more games while breaking the 20 game mark only once.

Sutton never pitched a no-hitter, but he did pitch five one-hitters and nine two-hitters. He was more of a control pitcher than a strikeout king, walking 80 or more batters only three in his career, and usually issuing around 50 to 60 free passes a season.

Sutton was tough in the postseason, although none of his teams ever won a World Series. He was 6-4 overall in post-season games, with 61 strikeouts in 100 innings.

LIFETIME STATS: W: 324, L: 256, Sv: 5, ERA: 3.26, SO: 3,574, CG: 178.

101. Rafael Corrales "Raffy" Palmeiro, 1B-OF-DH, Cubs, Rangers, Orioles, 1986–present.

Palmeiro was an underappreciated star in his three years with the Cubs, even though he hit .307 in his first full year and made the All Star team.

He was traded to Texas, and moved from the outfield to first base. After having some difficulties, Palmeiro found his groove and hit .319 in 1990 for the Rangers and .322 in 1991, making the All Star team again. He also led the league in doubles that season, with 49.

After slumping in 1992, Palmeiro bounced back in 1993, hitting .295 and scoring a league-leading 124 runs. He was traded to the Orioles, and hit .300 or better twice, and .289 or better twice in five years. He averaged 40 home runs a year for Baltimore from 1995-98.

Palmeiro eventually returned to the Rangers in 1999, and hit .324.

After struggling at first base initially, Palmeiro has been an effective fielder at first base. He won three consecutive Gold Gloves from 1997 to 1999.

Palmeiro is the active career leader in doubles, with 543, and 18th on the all-time list. His 528 home runs as of the beginning of the 2004 season place him 13th on the career list.

LIFETIME STATS: BA: .291, HR: 528, RBI: 1,687, H: 2,780, SB: 93.

Index